THE F
A NIGH
TELEVIS

The date was February 1, 1982. The show opened with an unidentified middle-aged man furtively warning viewers that they probably ought to tune out because the next sixty minutes might shock and repel them. Viewers who failed to heed the warning were then treated to a group of six somewhat sleazy chorus girls prancing around and waving tatty, colored feathers. They were introduced as the Rainbow Grill Peacock Girls; "You know spring is just around the corner when the Peacock Girls begin to moult." After this absurdly overblown introduction, David Letterman appeared on the stage in blue jeans and a sport jacket that seemed to have some trouble with the fit … Then he offered to take the audience on a tour of the fabulous set of *Late Night with David Letterman.* He tried to prepare viewers for the pressure-packed atmosphere of the control room, likening it to the command post of the air traffic controllers; when he finally opened the door, it was to reveal the staff drinking and reveling, and for some reason wearing Bavarian peasant costumes…

THE DAVID LETTERMAN STORY

By Caroline Latham

B

BERKLEY BOOKS, NEW YORK

Photographs in inset courtesy of
AP/Wide World Photos: pp. 1, 5, 7, 8;
Ball State University Press Service: p. 4.

This Berkley book contains the complete
text of the original hardcover edition.

THE DAVID LETTERMAN STORY

A Berkley Book / published by arrangement with
Franklin Watts

PRINTING HISTORY
Franklin Watts edition published 1987
Berkley edition / April 1988

ISBN: 0-425-10921-6

A BERKLEY BOOK ® TM 757,375
Berkley Books are published by The Berkley Publishing Group,
200 Madison Avenue, New York, NY 10016.
The name "BERKLEY" and the "B" logo
are trademarks belonging to Berkley Publishing Corporation.

PRINTED IN THE UNITED STATES OF AMERICA

10   9   8   7   6   5   4   3   2   1

Acknowledgments

A biography is necessarily a collaborative work, requiring the help of many other people. Among those who extended their cooperation and courtesy to me in the course of writing this book were: Tom Cochrun; Marilyn Dearing; John Eiden; Patricia Francis; Marie Fraser; Betsy Harris; Johnny Lieberbaum; Sidney Maurer; Tom Olvey; Debbie Paul; Ron Pearson; Krista Reese; Lou Sherman; and several others who prefer to remain anonymous.

I have also been helped enormously by previously published interviews with David Letterman and critical reviews of his work. I owe an especial debt to Tom Shales of the *Washington Post*, who has written often and well about David, as well as to Sam Merrill, whose interview with David appeared in *Playboy*, and Lewis Grossberger, who wrote two articles about David and *Late Night* for *Rolling Stone*. As usual, my researcher Jeff Sorenson deserves a vote of thanks for finding all these publications in the library—and waiting in line to get them photocopied.

My special thanks go to Libby and David Reddick for helping me find my way around Indianapolis (and keeping me well fed while I was doing it); to my aunt Shirley Scott for inspired sleuthing in Angola, Indiana; to the staff of The Publisher's Helper, always so much more than just typists; to Ed Breslin, who has been a helpful, responsive, and confident editor; and most of all to Alice Martell, agent extraordinaire.

Contents

Chapter One
About David Letterman . . . and You
1

Chapter Two
*Like Most People, David Letterman
Was Once a Child*
8

Chapter Three
Look Out, Ball State, Here Comes Dave
20

Chapter Four
Back Home in Indianapolis
38

Chapter Five
California Dreamin'
55

Chapter Six
A Show of One's Own
78

Chapter Seven
Letterman Redux
97

Chapter Eight
*He Gets by with a Little
Help from His Friends*
111

Chapter Nine
Giving and Taking Offense
131

Chapter Ten
*Does Anyone Know the
Real David Letterman?*
146

Chapter Eleven
*What Makes
David Letterman Funny?*
159

Chapter Twelve
Comparing the Incomparable
179

Chapter Thirteen
Whither David Letterman?
206

THE DAVID LETTERMAN STORY

Chapter

1

About David Letterman
. . . and You

Eddie Murphy says that *Late Night with David Letterman* is "the hippest thing on television." The wife of Canada's prime minister, Mila Mulroney, watches it every night. When the NBC affiliate in Baton Rouge made the mistake of taking the show off the air in 1983, students at Louisiana State University picketed the station and organized protests to gather petitions bearing thousands of names. According to a *Newsweek* cover story in February, 1986, the ratings for the show have improved to the point that NBC now uses *Late Night* to push its weaker programs, offering special rates for ads on the Letterman show to sponsors who will buy time on *Friday Night Videos* and other such fare.

But Larry "Bud" Melman says it best: "This show is the reason television was invented."

David Letterman, however, takes a more modest view. "We're not mining diamonds here," he told one interviewer. "It's rip and read, pure TV." He explains his concept of the show's appeal. "What we have is sort of found comedy. We take cameras into the street and do silly stuff. I tend to be cynical, which leaches into the finished show, if it can be called finished." Far be it from him to understand why all those people are actually watching the show. "*Late Night* is just something they have to get used to," he muses.

Behind the genuine modesty lies a genuine ambition to create a television show that is truly different from the rest of the stuff on the medium. Does it seem to you that being covered with chips and then lowered into a vat of dip is just a silly stunt? David sees it as something more. "That sort of thing pierces the flatness of the television screen. It's great if you can get people to actually *talk* about something they saw on television. In the first years of television, that's all people did talk about, because there never had been television before. But now, heavens, we've just seen it all." Thus David turns to a kind of conceptual comedy that is a new way of looking at reality. "We do a lot of what we call 'found comedy.' Things that you find in newspapers. Viewer mail. The fact that January actually *is* National Soup Month, so we're saluting soup all this month. I don't know if this stuff is more funny, but I do know that I feel more comfortable dealing with something that's actually there than with some lame premise we cook up." Or, as one of David's staff writers put it, "We are always aware that we're an entertainment show, but the truth is, we keep in mind that any television entertainment spectacle is faintly ridiculous."

Although David is willing to undertake such stunts as dressing in a Velcro suit and leaping up against—and sticking to—a Velcro wall, he admits to a low threshold of embarrassment about such antics. His own self-image is of a broadcaster rather than a comedian. In fact, he doesn't even really like to perform comedy in front of an audience, which would be something of a drawback if he wanted a career as a comedian. "I don't have that undeniable performing instinct in my veins like some guys. Robin Williams or Richard Pryor, they would get onstage six, seven times a night, as long as the electric bill was paid. I get up there and have to do twenty minutes, I'm gone in fifteen. . . . I don't go out there thinking, 'By God, I'm gonna get this crowd if I have to sweat out my $300 tuxedo.' "

In the same interview (with Larry Kart of the *Chicago Tribune*) David went on to say, "And I don't like the comedian image—the feeling that I'm the court jester who comes out after the banquet to make people laugh. I've had debates with my comedian friends about that. They say, 'What are you talking about? You can make huge sums of money as a comic.' And I say, 'You give me Shecky Greene or David Brinkley: which of the two is going to get more respect?' "

David's desire for respect is one reason he gave up his spot as a semiregular on NBC's prime-time show *TV's Bloopers and Practical Jokes*. No matter how good the ratings, or how high the fee for his appearances, the show was simply one he couldn't respect. In fact, it was uncomfortably like the things he enjoys poking fun at on his own program.

Not everyone gives David the respect he wants. When the going gets rough on *Late Night*, David quips, "I know you're saying, How'd that guy get a program? That's not *your* problem." To those who complain that his guests sometimes lack not only pizzazz but the ability to keep the viewers awake, David says, "I think it's important to have guests who annoy the public. It feels good to scream at the TV once in a while, to go to work the next day and tell everyone how annoyed you are."

Occasionally, criticism finds him too surprised to respond. In May 1986 he finally had Cher on the program, after asking her for four years to be his guest. He took the risk of asking her why she had finally changed her no to a yes. She answered, with her usual candor, "I thought I would never want to do this show with you."

"Why?" probed David, playing with fire.

No response from Cher.

"Why?" persisted David. "Because you thought I . . . ?"

"Was an asshole," announced Cher.

There was a long silence from David, and finally he joked, "I think a lot of people feel that way about me."

He's probably right. For every die-hard fan of *Late Night*, there's someone who dislikes the show intensely. The reasons given run from "He's not funny" to "I'm not an American so I don't understand him" to "He has a crappy smile" to "He's sick." In other words, David Letterman is certainly not everyone's cup of tea. But those who do like him, do so intensely. They watch every night, they write for tickets to watch the tapings, they buy T-shirts to proclaim their devotion. An ambitious young man in Florida, Johnny Lieberbaum, sells *Late Night* T-shirts emblazoned with pictures of Dave, Paul Shaffer, Larry "Bud" Melman, and Chris Elliott; simply running a small ad in the classified section of *Rolling Stone* has turned his Dr. Ed Squid Productions into a thriving business overnight, and now he is expanding to bumper stickers, facial blotters, and collapsible cups. And his customers don't just send orders; they write letters, sharing their feelings about Dave and the rest of the *Late Night* crew. With Michael Jackson in hiding to protect himself from germs and Prince worn out from months of prancing, David Letterman is the new hero. He's also, of course, a far more complex personality.

His status as a cult hero notwithstanding, David Letterman has remained a very private person. True to his Hoosier heritage, he is not fond of blowing his own whistle. In fact, he doesn't even want to be in the room when someone else is blowing it. Thus, as famous people go, relatively little is known about him personally. You may be a fan, but can you trace his dog Bob's pedigree? Name the grade school teacher who first doubted his future potential? Recognize the faces of his next-door neighbors even though they try to hide their shame?

No doubt your first impulse on hearing that a book about David Letterman is at last available—at a bookstore near you!—is to run right out and get hold of a copy. But try to remember that you are a busy person with no time to waste. Do you really *need* to read a book about David Letterman?

To answer that question, just take the following simple quiz. Be sure to keep track of your score. (Pencils and batteries are not included with this book.)

1. David Letterman grew up in

    (a) a trailer park
    (b) Indianapolis
    (c) a trailer park in Indianapolis
    (d) a daze.

2. David Letterman's first job in show business came in

    (a) 1969
    (b) a real dump
    (c) a freak accident that left no survivors
    (d) less time than it takes to tie your shoe.

3. David's big break came when

    (a) he was spotted by a talent scout for the Mous-
        keteers

   (b) he had his teeth capped to create that sexy gap

   (c) the woman agreed not to press charges

   (d) everyone else had gone home for the day.

4. Dave got his current job because

   (a) he was the best man for the job

   (b) he was the tallest man for the job

   (c) he was the only man who would take the job

   (d) the network was just too damned tired to care anymore.

5. Dave's secret desire is for

   (a) a home in the suburbs and 2.3 kids

   (b) Johnny Carson's time slot

   (c) a dog who can write his *own* funny lines

   (d) just one moment of sanity.

6. The secret of David Letterman's success is

   (a) hard work and great talent

   (b) an uncanny knack for pencil stalactiting

   (c) the secret tapes that he used to blackmail NBC

   (d) a plot by extraterrestrials to take over our planet.

Now it's time to score yourself. If your score is 90 points or more, you are a personal friend of Dave's, and have no business reading this book or any other. If your score is lower than 10, you are a loser who probably doesn't have the money to buy a newspaper, let alone a book. If you answered every question with (a), you have a sunny and optimistic personality that will make you popular with large dogs and lost tourists. If your answers form a pattern of a b b a c d c d, you have just written a sonnet. If there is no discernible pattern to your answers, you are a deeply confused individual who should be taken off the streets for your own good.

But enough about YOU. Let's get back to David Letterman.

Chapter

2

Like Most People, David Letterman Was Once a Child

Dave Letterman one wrote his own, highly imaginative, capsule bio. It began, "Mr. Letterman was born in the first double-wide mobile home manufactured in central Indiana, and is the only member of his family who did not go on to become a relative. David attributes his likable manner to those beginnings. Mr. Letterman not only has a college degree, but a high school one as well."

He also claims he always wanted to be a talk-show host.

It seems an oddly specific ambition for a child, doesn't it? But he told *Playboy*'s interviewer, apparently with a straight face, "At first it was just a vague vision of me on television with a few friends, drinking a warm eight-pack of beer and chatting about the week's events." That remains the spirit of *Late Night with David Letterman*, even if the format has become somewhat more sophisticated. But what kind of a kid would conceive of such a vision of his future?

All available information suggests that Dave was about the same when he was young as he is now that he's all grown up. If he had lived on your block, you wouldn't have paid him any special attention. He was just an ordinary kid with a shock of hair that was always threatening to break out into a cowlick, a gap-toothed grin, the usual boyish sense of mischief. He was never the class clown, didn't try to make himself the center of everyone's attention. But the people who knew him well knew that he could be funny. It wasn't that he knew a lot of jokes; it was just that he had a kind of humorous outlook on things. Dave likes to imply that his attitude was a matter of inheritance. "My mother's father was a very funny man—a real smartass, but irresistible. He'd have me sneak up on the watermelons because that was the only way you could pick them. So there would be this man in his sixties and me, a little kid, tiptoeing together through the watermelon patch, and we'd finally grab one and run like hell. My father was always joking around; and if she had a couple of beers, even my mom could get a little loopy."

Actually, life with the Lettermans sounds alarmingly wholesome.

Dave was born and raised in Indianapolis, one of the most pleasant but unremarkable of midwestern cities. Although it is the state capital of Indiana and has a total metropolitan population of over a million, Indianapolis retains a small-town feeling. Laid out in a hub over the flat, featureless land, the city consists of a number of separate and stable neighborhoods within the pie-shaped wedges, all encircled by a modern six-lane freeway. There are some big old houses that are still well kept up, and some very livable new ones with reasonable price tags for young families. There's a feeling of space, and plenty of trees. Kids ride their bikes to grade school, and neighbors greet them by name as they pass by. Even in high school, teachers probably know their parents and remember the exploits of their siblings. Indianapolis is a nice place to grow up.

As a young married couple, Joseph and Dorothy Letterman bought a small house in the section of the city called Broad Ripple, at that time still outside the city limits. Located in the middle of a block of square one-story houses on lots too narrow to provide much of a side yard, the Letterman house looked like the modest dream of the average American couple in the postwar period. Perhaps it was a bit crowded by the time all three children were growing up, but it remained a comfortable place to live, a home like the ones pictured in magazine ads of the 1950s and television shows of that more innocent era. David Letterman himself has likened the atmosphere to "a solid *Father Knows Best* or *Leave It to Beaver* type of lower-middle-class family."

Dave's parents were both children of former coal miners who had left the mines and turned to farming in rural Indiana. They were the kind of people who kept the same friends for an entire lifetime, who stayed close to their relatives, who went to church every Sunday and played an active role in the community. Joe Letterman had a flower shop in Broad Ripple and seems to have been a go-getter; he was the first FTD florist in the area. He is still remembered by the people in the area because of his habit of planting dogwoods as lavishly as he could afford to, along the streets, in parks, and in other people's yards; if Broad Ripple in the spring is a lovely sight, part of the credit goes to him. In the late 1950s, his business began to have problems, and Dave remembers that from then on, "there was a lot of financial tension around the house." We're not talking about poverty or anything dramatic . . . just the ordinary man's struggle to provide for his family a decent home, clothes that are in style, a summer vacation, and college educations for the kids.

David Michael Letterman was born in 1947, a middle child sandwiched in between two sisters. Dave was the kind of kid who liked to play outside all the daylight hours, shooting baskets, racing bikes, getting up to some minor mischief at the playground. In school, he impressed his teachers as obviously smart but not a particularly diligent student. He went to grade school at P.S. 55, just blocks away from his house. He was more or less indistinguishable from the other kids who walked to school along with him.

But as he got older, his sense of humor started to be a recognizable characteristic of young Dave Letterman. By the time he entered Broad Ripple High School in the fall of 1961, along with about 400 other freshmen, a lot of kids had learned that he was funny when you hung out with him. He could be something of a tease, quick with a quip or a retort. Even his classwork showed a sense of the bizarre. For example, when asked to write a theme in English class about a significant event in some person's life, he chose to write an ode to a man who had committed suicide by swallowing paper towels. It was the kind of response that makes a teacher wonder whether to give the kid an A+ for his creativity or send him off for immediate professional help.

Broad Ripple High in the 1960s was a typical suburban school, with a student population (less than 1 percent black) drawn from the immediate vicinity. It was the kind of place where the girls all belonged to a not-so-secret organization called the Cutie Pies and wore blue jumpers to school on Fridays as badges of identification. The boys had their own social clubs, and their Friday attire was white Levis. According to Mrs. Marilyn Dearing, who was the guidance counselor at Broad Ripple when Dave went to school there—and in fact can still be found in that same office—*Happy Days* could have been filmed at their school.

The president of the class of '65, Tom Olvey (now a prominent Indianapolis attorney), remembers it as a place where most kids took academics seriously, attended the school functions enthusiastically, and tried to stay out of trouble. Tom says the guys at Broad Ripple thought they were really raising hell when they filled a car with four boys and a six-pack and went driving around the neighborhood at nine or ten o'clock.

Dave remembers those days of cruising and drinking warm beer fondly. But his comments reveal that high school was probably not his favorite place. "I was looking through my high school yearbook lately," he told *Playboy*. "We all looked like guys who'd be hanging around with John Hinckley. I mean, basically, *everybody* in high school looks like a duck."

What you conclude about how David Letterman fit into this world of duck look-alikes depends on who you talk to. His peers seem to recall someone who was just one of the guys. He was too shy to perform in public, but in private he could make everyone laugh. He was a member of one of the boys' social clubs, which was a group of fifty or sixty boys who got together for occasional parties but mainly just appreciated the feeling of some sort of belonging. "Dave's sense of humor was the same then as it is now," says Tom Olvey. "We all thought he was funny then."

Well, not quite all. If you talk to people who observed Dave from across the generation gap, you get a different story. "I didn't think David was funny then, and I still don't think he's funny," says Mrs. Dearing. She claims he went through Broad Ripple High as a nonentity, "a run-of-the-mill ordinary average kid," although his test scores showed that he had a lot more ability than he used. If Dave Letterman was recognized at all by the adults at Broad Ripple High, it was largely because his father was the president of the school's Association of Parents and Teachers, and his sister Gretchen was quite a good student.

David himself frankly admits that his years at Broad Ripple High were "not the best time of my life. I was very shy." In an interview for *Indianapolis Monthly* with its editor in chief (his Broad Ripple High classmate Debbie Dorman Paul), he assessed himself candidly. "I was not good in math or chemistry and I realized athletics were not going to make me wealthy. The only thing that came easily to me was English—writing and public speaking. I started to think, 'Is there any way that I can practically apply this to my life?' I mean, outside of shop, that's pretty rare." He had signed up for speech class because he'd heard it was an easy C, and it turned out that he actually enjoyed it.

For anyone familiar with midwestern life in the 1960s, it's pretty easy to reconstruct David Letterman's life as a high school student. He had two really close friends he spent a lot of time with, Fred Stark and Steve Browne; the trio went everywhere together. Interestingly, many people who knew the boys then say that Fred, not Dave, is the one they would have predicted would go on to fame and success. Dave's participation in school activities was somewhat marginal. Although he loved sports, his only actual team membership during high school was on the freshman basketball team and the freshman reserve track team. He was in the band for two years, and for two years he was in "Ripples," a school organization whose raison-d'être was to put on a funny show once a year. It's just where you'd expect a young David Letterman to shine, but he thought performing in public was too nerve-wracking. Apparently he never even wrote a skit that was accepted for the show, and Mrs. Dearing says that when they handed out points for participation at the end of the production, Dave got only one. As far as school officials were concerned, Dave's greatest achievement at Broad Ripple was the fact that he was a hall monitor for all four years. Yes, David Letterman was actually a dedicated hall monitor, preserving law and order in the corridors of his high school.

Most of the kids who knew Dave Letterman liked him, but one can deduce that he was not considered one of the really "popular" students at Broad Ripple—a fact that probably helped his development as a comic. It's hard to imagine a prom queen or football hero going on to earn a living being funny. People who feel totally successful in their teens don't need to develop a sense of humor, and most likely couldn't step clear of their satisfying social environment to see the funny side of it; they don't, or can't, acquire the indispensable ironic distance. The best comedians tend to stand slightly outside the charmed circle of acceptance, just far enough away to gain a sense of perspective. (Too great a distance often brings its own distorting bitterness or humiliation.) To be totally accepted is to enter into a social contract that makes it difficult to point out flaws or shortcomings, even in a humorous way.

In a *Rolling Stone* interview, Dave explained to journalist Lewis Grossberger how he saw his situation in high school. "I never had a whole lot of friends, but I was in the group of people that was always making fun of everybody else. You know, we weren't in the honor society, so we made fun of the honor society. And yet we weren't the guys stealing cars, so we made fun of the guys stealing cars. We couldn't do much. My grades weren't good, and the guys I hung out with, their grades weren't really good. And we couldn't go out with the really good-looking girls. We would egg their houses. We'd find the best-looking girl and without ever *asking* her out—we'd just assume she wouldn't go out—we'd just go egg her house on theory, you know, just, hell, 'Screw you, I *know* you're not gonna go out with me, so we'll egg your house.' " That impulse remains the basis of some of David Letterman's most successful humor. He says that later on he just learned to do the same thing with his mouth—no need to buy the eggs.

We can deduce that Dave didn't have really fond memories of his high school years because he never returned to Broad Ripple after he became famous. Whereas he remains loyal to his college alma mater, and mentions it often, and still regards himself as a real Hoosier, he seems to have severed his connection with Broad Ripple High School. Officials say he has never offered to contribute anything to the school, not even an open letter to the students. Fellow alums of the class of 1965 had hoped he would attend the twenty-year reunion in 1985. One of them wrote about the attempt to find out whether or not he would come. "Our most famous classmate being a sort of superstar and all, we'd inquired as to the possibility of his attending. . . . One memory of the gap-toothed, freckled redhead who grouped himself tightly with three guys now about as famous as the rest of us consists of an 11 a.m. lunch line wherein the foursome would, in baritoned revelry, imitate disc jockeys on WIBC. . . . From that, a somebody was born—a superstar with an agent, a publicist, a manager and a secretary who says she'll give him the message. The bottom line is that after a couple of letters went unanswered, a leftover geometry teacher best remembered for wearing chalk smears around his mouth was a guest in the audience of Dave's show and managed a brief visit with him afterward and gave him our request. Dave'll let us know." Somehow, it wasn't really a surprise when Dave didn't show for the reunion.

Perhaps one reason Dave stood a little outside the in-group social whirl at Broad Ripple High was that he didn't have a lot of time for it. All four years there he worked after school at a local grocery store, the Atlas Super Market. The store is an Indianapolis institution, an independently owned grocery filled to bursting with an amazing variety of gourmet items such as beautifully trimmed crown roast of lamb, the best water-packed tuna from Japan, locally made jams and jellies, chocolates from around the world. Presiding over this astonishingly exotic assortment of foodstuffs is owner Sidney Maurer, a man who lives and breathes his work. He generally employs six to eight kids in his store, and treats them like a stern-talking uncle who can't quite conceal his heart of gold.

Sid remembers Dave as a good kid. "He was always here when I needed him," he explained approvingly. Like all the kids who worked at Atlas, Dave got the job by coming in to fill out an application and having an interview with Sid to tell him why he wanted the job. Sid knew the Letterman family, because Joe Letterman was a fellow merchant in the area. But he makes it a point never to hire anyone just because his parents make the request. He wants to make sure the kid has the gumption to come in and ask for the job himself.

Dave's first job was learning to sack groceries and carry them out to customer's cars. ("Our store is only as strong as the carry-out boy," warns Sid.) After mastering those skills, he advanced to stocking shelves, cleaning the store, and helping out wherever things were getting busy. He made deliveries and was trusted to take cash deposits to the bank. Eventually, he made it all the way to the top—and was allowed to preside over a cash register.

It was almost a family atmosphere at the Atlas, thanks in large part to Sid's attitude toward his young employees; as he puts it, "We're proud of all our kids." Dave often worked with fellow classmate Jeff Eshowsky, and there was always time for a little horsing around. Dave has told

the story of how he and the other guys at the store occasionally made off with a six-pack of beer they sneaked
out the back door and picked up as they left work. Sid
says he was aware it was happening but turned a blind
eye because his loss wasn't frequent or big enough to be
a problem; he saw it as the prank it was. Sid smiles as
he tells about how Dave used to like to tease the store
manager, a middle-aged man "straight as a post." One
of his jokes, in response to being asked to stack up a
display of coffee cans in the aisle, was to build the pile
all the way to the ceiling, thus defeating any possible
attempt by a customer to remove a can for purchase. Says
Sid matter-of-factly, "In the store, not everyone appreciated his humor." During those high school years, someone took a snapshot of Dave and Jeff on the job, standing
in the freezer with the meat. Dave is caressing a leg of
beef and, to judge from the gleam in his eye, possibly
contemplating doing something obscene with it.

Dave still likes to talk about his stint at the Atlas Super
Market. Did you happen to catch the show on which he
brought in some kid currently working at a grocery check-
out counter and challenged him to a grocery-sacking contest? According to Sid, Dave still bags his own groceries
when he goes shopping. And it says something about the
camaraderie of the place that not only did Dave work
there all through high school and during vacations of his
first few years of college, he also shopped there after he
finished college and moved back to Indianapolis with his
wife.

It is possible that Dave particularly enjoyed being
around Sid Maurer, with his very paternal attitude of
demanding benevolence, because his own father was very
ill at the time. Joe Letterman, that hardworking pillar of
the community, had a heart attack when Dave was still
in high school and died a few years later, in his forties.

Later Dave was able to joke about it, as he was about everything; explaining his family background to some interviewer, he quipped, "My mother's still working, but my dad is dead, so he does precious little anymore." But at the time, everyone who knew the family agreed Dave was emotionally shaken. And why not? It's a bad time for a boy to lose a father, just when he most needed the opportunity to be recognized as his father's peer. Like most boys in that place and time, David Letterman grew up respecting his father and hoping to win his good opinion. People who knew the family say Joseph Letterman sometimes worried about his son: Dave was a nice boy but a little *different*. Would he learn to use that difference to his advantage, or would it stand in his way? It must not have been easy for Dave to lose his father before he knew the answer to that question.

So maybe Dave Letterman had a little more on his mind than some of his classmates. But when he lined up with the 394 other students who made up the class of 1965 at Broad Ripple High School, he was basically just another face in the crowd. He was tall, a little bit skinny and gangly, looking out at the world through his heavy-rimmed glasses with a somewhat jaundiced view. He went everywhere on his bike or in friends' cars, never having a car of his own until he was in college. He was interested in girls but he didn't date much, and no one can remember any one girl who was special for him. He was mentioned in the Class Prophecy, but only for what struck his classmates as an odd anatomical feature: "There stood Dave Letterman, just as bowlegged as ever because of his career as a professional cowboy." His grades were mostly C's, not good enough for his ability and not nearly as good as his sisters' grades—but not so terrible either. His life-long interest in sports was already in full bloom, but he had no illusions about himself as more than an amateur participant. He looked about as old then as he does now, with one of those faces that is perenially boyish without ever looking really young. He loved his family but didn't feel it was necessary to confide in them about his feelings. He had some good friends, with whom he could be himself and have a good time. His ambitions were nebulous: like a lot of boys his age, he hoped he'd be able to find some kind of work that wasn't too hard or too boring and be able to earn a decent living doing it. As he put it to a *Rolling Stone* interviewer, "You don't need to be doing something that involves *heavy lifting*. Don't look for that kind of work. Look for something you can do easily." Heaven knows, you can't accuse young Dave of overweening ambition.

Chapter

3

Look Out, Ball State, Here Comes Dave

In the spring of 1986, a talented and hardworking young man explains why he decided to enroll in the radio and television department at Ball State University in Muncie, Indiana. "I know David Letterman went to school here. . . . I'm just hoping that some of whatever worked so well for him will rub off on me."

This already sounds like a setup for a joke. Especially considering that in high school, David Letterman was neither a very diligent nor a very interested student. His intention was to make it through college in the same desirable state.

He had originally hoped to go to Indiana University at Bloomington, a big state school and a good one, and the place his friends were going. But his grades just weren't good enough to get him in except on academic probation. "I'd have had to maintain a C average my freshman year and I figured, there's no way I can do that." So he applied to Ball State University, also part of the state system and located in nearby Muncie, just a little more than an hour's drive from Indianapolis. Ball State accepted him, and he entered in the fall of 1965.

Ball State is the concept of the university reduced to its simplest possible form. It was originally a state teacher's college, named after the benefactor who manufactured Ball canning jars nearby. (The company is now in aerospace technology.) It was promoted to the status of University only a few years before David Letterman enrolled, but the new title doesn't seem to have brought much change. At that time, Muncie had a population of about 50,000 people living on flat farmland located over a big pocket of natural gas. The gas brought some industry to the area and is probably the reason Muncie grew while other towns around it remained small agricultural communities.

An interesting sidelight on Muncie is that it was the location of a classic sociological study called *Middletown*. Robert and Helen Lynd undertook the extensive study during the 1920s; it covered economics, home and family life, leisure time activities. "Middletown" was a place where families spent weekends walking and picnicking in the two parks, where bowling and drinking beer in taverns were popular activities for men while their womenfolk patronized the bookmobile and went window-shopping on the main street. Some folks said the local religion was high school basketball, and the fate of the Muncie Central Bearcats still occupies the minds of Muncie residents, with divorcing couples haggling in court over custody of the season tickets.

The Lynds found that there were really only two significant social classes in Middletown, the workers and the managers—and the gulf between them was vast. Followup studies indicate it's still that way today. Recent comparisons of Muncie then and Muncie now suggest not much has changed in the intervening sixty years. Rolf Meyersohn, a sociologist at the City University of New York, is one of the researchers who has recently taken a second look at Middletown. "The changes in leisure have been less than one had dreamed. It's disappointing to people who thought there would be some brave new world. In the 1920s, Muncie as "Middletown" symbolized middle-class, midwestern, middle *everything* in America. That hasn't changed either."

The campus of Ball State is stretched out one building deep along several blocks of Muncie's two main downtown streets. Most of the buildings date from the 1940s, '50s, and '60s, decent utilitarian structures with little style or individuality. Only the presence of a couple of bookstores and more than the usual quota of pizza places in the commercial blocks gives any hint that Muncie is a college town. It lacks the natural food store, the friendly little shops with trendy clothes, the "nice" jewelry store with suitable Christmas presents for Mom and a selection of ever so small diamond rings for the newly engaged—all the clutter of businesses that usually cater to student tastes and means. You get the impression that Ball State students don't have a whole lot of extra spending money, and that their college life is not so important to them that they want to embellish it with a lot of purchases.

Although Ball State was already a university in Dave's day, it was still small enough to allow professors to know most of the students in their department and for classmates to know a lot about one another. There are some good and committed teachers at Ball State, but perhaps the school's greatest virtue was summarized by one of the faculty in talking about famous former student Letterman: "We do our best job here when we don't destroy what they have coming in before we let them out."

That's what Ball State did for David Letterman, and

he remains grateful. Whatever he may or may not have learned in the classroom, the school gave him the opportunity to find out what he could do best, and some confidence in his ability to do it.

When it came time to declare a major, Dave opted for radio and television. Perhaps the choice was based on his childhood ambition to be on television drinking warm beer and talking to his buddies. He gave interviewer Bill Zehme a slightly different reason. "I was not a very good student. Then I got into this speech class and I realized that public speaking came easily to me. I thought to myself, 'Well, this is great. I don't have to work very hard and I get pretty good grades at it.' "

Ten years after he graduated from Ball State, someone asked Dave Letterman to sum up the school in three words. "No big deal," he quipped. He told another interviewer that attending Ball State was like spending four years at Michigan City (the Indiana state prison). But on a somewhat more serious note, he concluded, "Ball State was a place where you could have fun and not get arrested. It was a good experience. It was a nice place to grow up." He characterized his college years as a time of social maturation. He added, "Radio and TV were perfect for me. A lot of people come to study to be a teacher and then have trouble finding a teaching job. Some study animal husbandry, and there are very few animals who need husbands. But for me it was just practical experience, and I was able to turn it into a career." His final word on the subject: "So I have no doubts about the benefits of being at Ball State."

Today Ball State returns the compliment, officially taking the position that it has no doubts about the benefits of having had David Letterman in the Ball State student body. But there is some indication that not everyone was quite so doubt-free at the time he was actually there. His grades were never really a problem. He maintained a B average during his first two years of college, and even though that average slipped during the remaining two years, he was still academically adequate. But he was, let's face it, just a little bit flaky.

To demonstrate, ask the people who were involved with the student radio station, WBST, what they remember about David Letterman. They'll tell you that he was "an administrative problem." Dave started to work at the station just about the time it got a new manager, John Eiden. John's mission was to ride herd on the entire operation, which at that time was an extremely amateurish attempt to send 10 watts of oddly assorted programming into nearby student dorms. WBST played mostly classical music (any albums of popular music sent to the station were quickly appropriated by the staff, thus never making their way into the station's library). When they could afford it, they bought it all prepackaged and complete with suggested commentary. Student DJs were hired for $1.25 an hour, and they weren't expected to be able to do much except manage to pronounce the name of the composer and the piece. In fact, it wasn't taken for granted they could do even that: students were expected to listen to tapes in which a sonorous baritone continually repeated the correct pronunciation of the names of classical composers: "Show-pan . . . Show-pan . . . Show-pan."

John was supposed to impose stricter order on the station, to make it a more realistic learning experience for the students. He eventually achieved this goal, although not without a struggle, and today the station (still under John's management) is one that any telecommunications department might envy. Back in 1967, John was aided in his task by the student program manager, who had been chosen by the department's faculty. They picked Tom Watson, a bright and ambitious young man who went on to manage research at CBS and write a book on *I Love Lucy*. Watson was determined to put an end to the horseplay that went on not just in the studios of WBST but also on its airwaves.

Tom Watson considered DJ Dave Letterman one of his problems. Dave's time slot was the sign-on show that ran from noon till 3 p.m. Unfortunately, he was frequently late; as Dave himself later admitted, "I wasn't a very reliable employee." He sneaked forbidden cigarettes into the studio. Moreover, he didn't take his job of announcing classical music selections very seriously. In fact, he didn't even like classical music, but as John Eiden explained, Dave's position was that if someone was willing to pay him a buck and a quarter an hour, he'd play whatever the student programmer, a girl named Cheryl, had scheduled. Still, he thought he ought to be able to please himself occasionally too. He said later in an interview, "I used to have a radio program on WBST and that was just the best. That was my first outlet, my first place to just go and talk, and I loved it." But Program Manager Tom Watson became more and more irritated by Dave's attempts to inject his own personality into his classical music show. John Eiden says, "Dave was extremely creative, but not in the way Tom Watson wanted him to be."

Matters came to a head one fatal day when Dave was slated to play *Clair de Lune*. He announced the selection and then couldn't resist adding confidentially to his listeners, "You know the de Lune sisters. There was Clair, there was Mabel. . . ." An outraged Tom Watson, who had been monitoring the program, stormed into Eiden's office and demanded, "We've got to get rid of him." They did.

But he didn't leave the Muncie airwaves entirely. In a men's dorm called Wagner Hall, students were operating a pirate radio station, WAGO, from a disused broom closet. With all the power of 5 watts, the signal sometimes didn't even reach every room in the dorm, but its casual format and popular music made it a hit with those who were able to find it on their sets. One day the pretty receptionist at the dorm's front desk told one of the guys running the station that her boyfriend was a better DJ than anybody on WAGO. A few days later, Dave dropped by and did some stuff on the air, and sure enough, he *was* good. Although the station was not well enough organized to give anyone a regular slot, Dave frequently showed up to take over for a few hours. In general, WAGO relied heavily on blue humor, and Dave made halfhearted attempts in that direction. But it was clear that he was uncomfortable with it, and he's never used blue humor since.

Dave's years at Ball State were a time that he cut loose. He spent a lot of time just amusing himself, sitting around with some like-minded spirits, drinking beer out of long-necked bottles and kidding each other mercilessly. They all liked to make jokes about Muncie (which was probably where Dave's later comparison of living in the town with a stint in Michigan City prison came from). One of Dave's favorite targets was a society columnist for the town paper, the *Muncie Evening Press*. He liked, for example, to joke that she had invented the all-but-lethal wrestling hold known as the "Muncie Evening Press," and got a kick out of describing her ferocious application of the hold on various occasions.

In retrospect, Dave remembers there was a lot of drinking and fooling around. "The big thing was to get as drunk as possible as early in the day as possible so you would be conscious for the least amount of time. College enables young people to be stupider longer with minimal jeopardy. In fact, that was on the shield of my fraternity in Latin: 'Stupider Longer.' " In a *Playboy* interview, he discussed this aspect of his college career in more detail. "In college, my friends and I pretty much structured our week around obtaining beer for the weekend. We loved almost every aspect of drinking beer, particularly the fact that we could physically get away with it. One of the remarkable things about being nineteen is that you can break open a case of warm beer at midnight and still be wide-eyed and alert for your 8 a.m. class. And that gave me the false impression that my life would always be like that."

Although the time was the turbulent 1960s, when students were burning their draft cards and dumping pig's blood—or worse—over the campus buildings, and eventually making Lyndon Johnson afraid to run again for the presidency, Ball State was largely untouched by these trends. "We were amazingly isolated," recalls David. "I was only vaguely aware of the political turmoil of the time. . . . It was a lot different from being at Berkeley. All I was concerned about was buying a station wagon and getting married." He adds, "I was hardly aware of the Vietnam War until a friend of mine flunked out and was drafted and was dead like that. One day, here's a guy setting fire to the housemother's panty hose, and the next day he's gone. *That* got my attention."

But Dave didn't worry about world affairs all the time. A friend of the time describes him as being a basically conscientious person who occasionally took liberties in having fun during his college career. One of his former professors remembers that there was frequently a small crowd around Letterman outside the classroom door. "I noticed that the students were always laughing and whenever he stopped to talk, there would be a circle around him." Another informant says Dave was always one of the guys when it came to creating a little diversion. He tells of a field trip the radio and television majors took to

New York to see CBS, under the sponsorship of the then
head of the department, Dr. Tomlinson, a former employee of CBS. "On the train trip back to Indiana, Dave
and some other guys got off somewhere in darkest Ohio,
got snockered and almost missed the train. Dr. T. was
not too pleased."

Rumor has it that Dave was not the best of students,
even in a department that wasn't known for enforcing
really tough standards. In fact, some people would have
you believe Dave didn't even actually *graduate*, a myth
possibly fueled by the absence of a senior class picture to
prove he was there (and virtually no pictures of him at
all in the college yearbook). But at least one member of
the teaching staff leaps to his former student's defense.
"I had him in several classes," Dr. Darrell Wible is quoted
as saying in a Ball State news bureau release, "starting
with mass communication class when he was a freshman
in 1966. The class had seventy-five students. He always
had the answers to the questions—no comedic stuff—
and he was one of only four or five who made an A."
Wible, a former sportscaster and local radio station manager before he entered academia, did go on to add somewhat apologetically, "After that, he discovered the thrill
of being on the air and his scholarly work suffered ac-
cordingly."

Dave is modest in his own evaluation of his academic
career. He told a group of students when he went back
for the 1979 homecoming that "school was not a breeze
for me. Coming back to campus has produced some anxiety for me. I remember sneaking into classes late in this
very building." His college memories include forgetting
a term paper due the next day, suddenly discovering that
the radio show he'd prepared was six minutes too long,
and constantly worrying about grades. Dave thanked Dr.
Wible for his contribution to Dave's Ball State education:

"He did a lot for me by just looking the other way while I was screwing up. I appreciated that. It motivated me." He concluded pointedly, "My *outside-of-classroom* experiences here were valuable."

One of his most significant outside-of-classroom experiences at Ball State was falling in love and getting married. He met Michelle Cook early in his college career, and it was a serious relationship right from the beginning. Michelle was a music major, tall (nearly 6 feet) and attractive, a rather quiet young woman considered by those who know her to have a gracious personality and innate good taste. Dave lovingly subjected her to a barrage of tall jokes, teasing her about being a tree in the university arboretum, Christy Wood, or working as the light-bulb changer in the school gym. Michelle responded by acting as Dave's biggest fan and booster. A family friend recalls that they were "madly in love" and they finally decided to get married while they were still in school.

Such a big step of course brought financial responsibilities, which they both worked to meet. Michelle labored as a waitress in a local eatery, and Dave succeeded in getting hired by a real radio station in Muncie, WERK. He got the job by starting as a substitute for the regular man on the shift, Tom Cochrun. Tom, who is currently the news anchor and award-winning documentary producer/correspondent for WTHR-TV in Indianapolis, had often seen Dave around the campus of Ball State, where they were both students. He remembered the job Dave did emceeing a big variety show his frat sponsored and thought he was "genuinely funny," irreverent and off the wall. So he suggested Dave as his replacement while he went to Europe, and Dave got the job. He played records and read the news, and apparently did a satisfactory job with both tasks. He was probably too anxious to hold onto the job to risk indulging his sense of humor.

Dave's success at WERK was soon parlayed into a summer job as a bench announcer at the ABC affiliate in Indianapolis, WLWI-TV (Channel 13). Dave explained his weighty responsibilities to journalist David Gritten. "Every half hour, I'd give the station's call sign and also announced every public service message." He added, "I thought it was terrific—here I was at nineteen, talking to central Indiana." With a typical self-deprecating grin, he added, "Of course, central Indiana wasn't listening." But it was good experience for him and later led to his first full-time professional job in broadcasting. Meanwhile, it helped to support him and his wife.

After he was a famous alumnus, someone asked David Letterman for his advice to Ball State communications students. Lord knows, it was the perfect setup for his wry humor, but he opted for a serious answer, and it gives a good indication of what he himself found most valuable about his years at Ball State. "Take advantage of everything available to you. Do as much as you can to understand all of the equipment. Anything you have a remote interest in, pursue it. Stay there until you've gotten everything you can out of the place before you go on, and don't sell those experiences short, because five or six years down the road they are going to be invaluable to you."

Among Dave's most interesting experiences at the time was his attempt to form a performing comedy group. It was called the Dirty Laundry Company, and most of the material was written by Dave. He was also one of the performers, and he succeeded in pressing Michelle into the act as well. The other two members of the troupe were fellow radio and television majors Ron Pearson, now the head of his own very successful ad agency in Indianapolis, and Joyce DeWitt, later to become one of the costars of *Three's Company*.

The Dirty Laundry Company first performed at a university homecoming program, with a mixture of skits and monologues by Dave that Ron Pearson says was almost like a Second City act. There was no blue humor, but there were a few jokes about drugs, including a bit that had everyone in the art department attempting to smoke their crayons. Ron recalls that the final skit was something called "The Dating Shame" with Joyce DeWitt as the contestant trying to choose between Bachelors Number One, Two, and Three. Her first choice was the suavely perfect guy played by Ron Pearson. But when he gets his first look at her, he declines to accept the date. The man who was her second choice turned out to be gay, and he walked off the program trying to get a date with Mr. Perfect. Finally she was left with no choice except Bachelor Number Three, another student named Mike Little, who had been affectionately dubbed "Fatty No-Neck" by Dave. Mike was wearing overalls and scratching himself in embarrassing anatomical locations. He too finally turned down poor Joyce, in favor of what seemed to be a lewd interest in one of his farm animals. Yes, it sounds a bit sophomoric, but then, you must remember, so was the audience. In any case, the entertainment was well received, and they got a few other engagements in the area. The president of a bank in nearby Marion asked the group to entertain at the annual Christmas party, an occasion on which Dave did a long monologue that included a number of jokes about the local area, which died as they emerged from his mouth. For this and other gigs, each member of the Dirty Laundry Company received a sum that Ron Pearson estimates to have been almost as much as $20.

Encouraged by what seemed to them like success (what did they know?) the group decided to go for the big time and audition for Indianapolis's Black Curtain Dinner Theater. It was a somewhat run-down old building, located in a shabby neighborhood, but it was about the only place in the city at that time that featured any kind of live comedy. Alas, the audition got off to an inauspicious start. In those days, Dave had a habit of referring to everyone as "that clown," and his friends and associates had picked up the locution. So when they arrived at the theater, Ron made the mistake of asking a fellow in overalls working outside at some maintenance task, "Can you tell me where to find the clown who runs this thing?" Back came the laconic answer, "I'm the clown you're looking for." Needless to say, their audition performance was viewed in dead silence, and silence continued to be the only response the Dirty Laundry Company ever got from the Black Curtain Dinner Theater.

Although the comedy group died a natural death from lack of opportunity to perform, the members remained friends, and they tried to coordinate their schedules so they took many of their classes at the same time. In one of their courses, each student was required to write, direct, and produce a half-hour radio show as a final project. Dave elected to do his in a talk show format (yes, folks, the Hand of Fate), which he called "The Uncle Gimpy Show." The program began with Dave, in his best slick announcer voice, saying persuasively, "Hey, kids, close all the windows and turn on the gas . . . it's 'The Uncle Gimpy Show.' " It has to be admitted that some of the jokes were downright painful. For example, Joyce DeWitt, playing the part of a female convict appearing as a guest on the show, explains to Uncle Gimpy (played by Ron Pearson) how she escaped: "I ate so much that I finally broke out."

But it's interesting to see, even in this very early stage of his career, Dave experimenting with some of the techniques he would later use on television. The way the program ended was crucially important to the grade it received; you could get an A only if your program ended *exactly* at the right second. When Dave's finished tape was played for the class, it appeared at first that he had blundered badly in this regard. With nearly five minutes to go, the background music started to rise as Dave in his announcer's voice began to recite the credits. Fellow students all over the room were nudging one another in the ribs and whispering about Dave's failure. Then suddenly they heard Dave in his everyday voice shouting at the guy in the control booth (a fiction, of course). *"Will you turn that music down?"* he asks in exasperation. He goes on trying to finish the credits and suddenly the music comes in again, played at a distortingly fast speed. Once again there is an angry explosion from Dave. This trouble with the imaginary guy in the control booth continues to hamper the final credits until Dave exhaustedly concludes them just as the hand sweeps over the correct second. The class was laughing and applauding because they knew Dave had skillfully manipulated their response.

What's interesting about this project, aside from Dave's ability to inflict real surprise on his fellow students, is his determination to remind listeners how the show is actually created. In the typical radio program, the audience is expected to take the background music as a given. They are not expected to think about how it got there, who is playing the tape, how he knew the correct volume at which to play it. The goal of most professional broadcasts is to make such elements seem so inevitable that they are never questioned. David Letterman's goal was and is to make the audience acutely aware of every one of these elements—and the people responsible for them. He wants the audience to remember there's someone sitting in the control booth who is playing that tape, fiddling with the volume knob, and possibly even, for reasons that are purely personal, attempting to make the announcer look bad.

Of course, part of his interest in showing us what goes on behind the scenes is rooted in the humorous possibilities. "The Uncle Gimpy Show," for example, also featured a report from the mobile unit, but when the unit was supposed to go on the air, it was in the process of becoming involved in a traffic accident. But there is also a philosophical aspect to this interest in revealing the reality behind the smooth on-the-air image. Some of David Letterman's best TV shows remind you of the scene in *The Wizard of Oz* when Toto goes behind a curtain in the Emerald Palace and reveals that the magnificent and all-powerful Wizard is actually a nervous little man from Kansas employing a couple of cheap mechanical gadgets. He likes to remind his viewers not to take the Wizard's tricks at face value; there's always a little man from Kansas lurking somewhere out of sight. Come to think of it, that must be the explanation for the continual presence of Larry "Bud" Melman on the show!

Dave graduated from Ball State in 1970. "What Ball State did," he later said appreciatively, "was teach me that it is possible to make a living in broadcasting." College had given him a little free time to play, some vocational training, and the chance to grow up. He was grateful, and he has expressed that gratitude in a number of ways. One was coming back to perform at the university homecoming in 1979 (with headliners The 5th Dimension). Another was the frequent—if mostly jocular—references to Ball State on his TV program. Says Dr. Wible, "That's the kind of free publicity that no university could ever afford to buy. It's priceless. Everyone hears the name Ball State."

The more time that goes by, the warmer seem to be

Muncie's recollections of David Letterman. His rather low visibility as a student has been more than compensated for by his high profile as a celebrity alum. Press releases label him Ball State's highest paid graduate (while candidly admitting that "Ball State wasn't ready for Dave in the late sixties.") Dr. Wible proclaimed, "There were a few who weren't impressed, but I thought he was a creative genius." An additional accolade came from the town of Muncie itself. In 1985 they planned to put up a billboard along Interstate 69, the nearest major highway, to promote Muncie as a destination, and its message was "David Letterman Slept Here," along with a pillow inscribed with the initials BSU. (Presumably it was not intended as a comment on his college career.) The consultant who conceived this idea explained rather glumly, "As you might suspect, a community like Muncie kind of has to look long and hard to find things that you can call tourist attractions." It seems Dave's one-time presence was about the best they could come up with. And in fact, the billboard was never actually erected.

In 1985, Dave offered Ball State more tangible evidence of his gratitude for letting him have the chance to go his own way. It was announced that he was establishing an annual fully funded scholarship for a telecommunications major, as well as giving the department $24,285 to purchase audio and video equipment. It was pointedly explained that the scholarship would *not* be given for academic achievement (good to see that Dave remains true to his beliefs) but instead for "creativity." Applicants were to submit whatever they thought would provide convincing evidence of creative ability—tapes, scripts, plans for projects. As it turned out, so much creativity was thereby made manifest that Dave ended up giving scholarships to not one but two students for the 1985–86 academic year. One was for a comedy spoof of a detective series, the other for a production called "The Party Animal." One of the winners freely admitted that his "grades were in the basement."

The first winner of the David Letterman Scholarship, in 1985, was Tom Gulley. Now here's the part that's hard to believe. Tom Gulley is tall (six feet, five inches), he loves sports, he wears jeans and sneakers most of the time. He likes to make wisecracks; for example, when asked what he intended to do with the $5,015 cash award, he answered, "Party." Now does this remind you of anyone?

It did Darrell Wible. He commented, "Tom is in many ways like David—the same kind of thinking, the same kind of abilities. David was extremely bright, articulate, mentally quick, and a young man who showed promise. He was a C student only in those classes where he didn't care. Tom is the same, except that he wills some energy to things he doesn't like to do." Nevertheless, Dave has never met Tom, and he didn't participate in the judging of scholarship applicants; apparently the judges found this Letterman clone all by themselves.

Tom Gulley explained why he wanted to win the scholarship (aside from the money, of course). "Since David Letterman is my idol, when I heard about the scholarship, I said to myself, 'I have to have this.' I wanted to be the first one ever to get it." After the announcement, Dave sent Tom a telegram: "Congratulations, Thomas. Sorry I couldn't be there in person. As you know, I'm busy with the Geneva Summit." Tom wired back his thanks, concluding, "By the way, I am going to be at the Geneva Summit too. See you there."

Ball State was naturally appreciative of David's gesture toward his alma mater. The chairman of the telecommunications department, John Kurts, said, "The generous gifts from David Letterman will insure that young professionals will continue to receive hands-on experience with state-of-the-art equipment. The scholarship will enable someone with excellent professional potential to concentrate on developing that potential without worrying about tuition, fees and other expenses. He has made an outstanding contribution to our program."

If you visit Ball State today, you can see the studio that is the result of David Letterman's gift. The telecommunications building (the very same one in which Dave worked and attended classes) has the much used look of any aging college building. Frequent rearrangements to try to get more efficient use from the space have left dirt marks on the floors from vanished furniture and revealed spots on the walls that weren't painted the last time around. In Dave's day, the dominant color was a blue-gray, the color of a lake before it rains; now the walls are an unmistakably institutional shade of turquoise. The older studios have been abandoned or turned into classrooms, including the one in which Dave told the world about the de Lune sisters. (It had been built rather strangely anyway, with the control booth constructed in such a way as to force the engineer to sit facing away from the studio where the show was being broadcast.) But now the department seems impressively equipped, and the studio that Dave's gift built certainly does look as if everything in it is state-of-the-art. Interestingly, the gift came complete with an aura of Dave's ironic attitude. Right outside the studio there is screwed to the wall (grimy with the fingerprints of many classes of students) an imposing slab of wood, on which in turn is screwed an oversize bronze plaque. On it is the inscription "Dedicated to all the C students before and after me," with the rather formal signature of David M. Letterman. My oh my, as someone might put it, there's a commemorative gesture you won't soon forget.

Chapter

4

Back Home in Indianapolis

What do you do when you've just graduated from Ball State with a degree in radio and television and you like the idea of eating regularly?

You go back home to Indianapolis and look for a job in broadcasting.

Dave already had a foot in the door because of his summer job as a booth announcer at Channel 13. He later confessed to having the feeling that he hadn't exactly wowed the station management during his summer stint. Although he had hoped to please, he ended up doing pretty much what he wanted to, because he didn't think any real viewers were ever watching him anyway. And, he concluded, "If there was ever a problem, they could always say, 'Well, he's just some relief kid. Don't worry, he'll be gone in the fall.'"

He nevertheless cherished the hope he would be given a full-time permanent job after he graduated. What happened instead is that the station kept him on a temporary basis until they could find someone they liked better to replace him. For six months, he lived through the unpleasant experience of watching one candidate after another turn up to audition for the job that was so precariously his. But this story has a happy ending, because the program director never found anyone he wanted to hire. "I just sort of got it through attrition," explained Dave. The temporary job became permanent.

Dave and Michelle settled into the apartment they had found, in a double house not too far from the old Broad Ripple neighborhood. (That allowed them to do their grocery shopping at the Atlas Super Market.) Ron Pearson, who went to work in Indianapolis at about the same time, remembers the place as being in a neighborhood consisting almost exclusively of old people, and adds in amusement, "Dave always managed to choose out-of-the-way illogical places to live." And he opted for the unconventional in his mode of transportation as well. While other young couples were buying station wagons and sensible family cars, Dave and Michelle were riding bicycles all over Indianapolis. Most of the city is flat, so in that way it is a good place for cyclists. But it does get its share of rain, and it can be very snowy in the winter. However, people who knew Dave in those days are unanimous in their recollection that he always managed to get in to work on his bicycle, no matter what the weather was like.

In the beginning, Dave obviously loved his job in television. "It was just great, the best experience anybody could have," he told Debbie Paul. "It was like graduate school—maybe better." WLWI inadvertently gave Dave the opportunity to perfect his own brand of humor and learn how to get it across on the small screen. The assignments he drew were those traditionally given to beginners, such as hosting the late night movie, interviewing 4-H kids on a regular Saturday afternoon show, and substituting for the weatherman on the weekend news program. Dave took these time slots known to have relatively few viewers and gave them a heavy dose of his own personality—and warped perspective.

For example, the late night movie he retitled *Freeze-Dried Movies*. The program came on at 2 a.m. and showed what he recalls as "bad, bad, bad Oriental monster movies, sponsored by a place that sold bad, bad, bad Oriental pizza." Secure in the assumption that practically no one with any sense was watching the program, Dave used it as a format for his own ideas of broadcasting humor. He explains, "In between the movies, I'd goof around with a cast of regulars. We had a telethon to raise money for a washed-up fighter. We celebrated our tenth anniversary in the show's second week. One guy showed up at the station wearing a stupid suit, and we dragged him onto the show so people could see it." He also led the stagehands in food fights that were the highlights of the intermissions.

Another of Dave's assignments was the Saturday special dedicated to letting the folks of central Indiana know about the achievements of the kids in the 4-H club. Dave called the show *Clover Power*, and he claims that what he really did as host was make fun of little kids. "I mean, there's not much else you can do. You'd have a kid with a bad complexion plugging a cord into a socket watching a light bulb light up, and you had to talk to him for ten minutes about it. It was so unnatural, so you had to say, 'I'll be damned, you're kidding, it really lights up like that. . . .'" When a girl who came on the show to talk about knitting tried to explain that the stitch she was currently describing was "just like the first one, only backwards," Dave instructed her to turn around so the audience would understand it better. It sounds like *Clover Power* was a good training ground for some of the interviews Dave now does on *Late Night with David Letterman*. When, for example, he drops into a luncheonette near the NBC studios and chides the counterman for the mis-spellings on the sign advertising the daily specials, or asks a dry cleaner to tell the audience about the cleaning he has done for a celebrity client whose picture is in the window, the final product is probably very much like the interviews on *Clover Power* of rather dazed kids who are trying to explain how their collies herd sheep.

In Indianapolis, David Letterman is best remembered in his incarnation as a television weatherman—probably because more people watched the news than any of the other shows he appeared on. He took over the meteo-rological maps on the weekend, when the *real* weather-man had time off. (As Dave likes to put it, "In the event that harm came to the regular weatherman, I was just a heartbeat away.") His on-the-air irreverence was astound-ing. "You can only announce the weather, the highs and lows, so many times before you go insane. In my case, it took two weeks. I started clowning. I'd draw peculiar objects on the cloud maps and invent disasters in fictitious cities. I made up my own measurements for hail, and said hailstones the size of canned hams were falling." On an-other weather report, he announced that a tropical storm had just been upgraded to hurricane status and then con-gratulated the storm on its career advancement. When the map showed the little stars that symbolize snowflakes, he suggested that the folks at home might like to cut that portion out of their picture and use it to make doilies. One night Dave's national weather map unaccountably had the state of Georgia missing; he told his audience that the government had traded that state for the country of Iran, which would be placed in its slot. Even the daily temperature readings evoked hilarity. "Muncie, 42 . . . Anderson, 44 . . . ," he would intone. "Always a close game."

In recent months, *Late Night* viewers have had the

opportunity to see for themselves what David Letterman looked like when he was Channel 13's weatherman. When Diane Sawyer was a guest on the show in spring 1986, she set the *60 Minutes* research team to work digging into David's past. The result was a set of photographs from those early days on television that had the studio audience in hysterics. The David Letterman of the early 1970s was a nerd in glasses with a thick wad of hair plastered down on top of his head that looked almost like some creature had made a home there. His clothes were "mod," with contrasting strong patterns, a far cry from his preppy look of today (maybe he learned something from all those Harvard guys in his writing staff). The total effect made Dave cringe and claim the photos actually showed his half-brother Earl, rather than him. Diane Sawyer smiled sweetly at his embarrassment and then concluded with a zinger: "It just proves what you can triumph over in life."

Indiana is a farming state and takes its weather seriously, and many of Dave's listeners were not amused by his antics. "People got disgusted and complained. . . . I was asked to tone it down a bit, but when the concept of 'happy news' came filtering across the country from New York, the station did a complete turnabout." Dave sums up the prevailing attitude toward his performance as a weatherman: "People said, 'Who is this punk and why is he making fun of the relative humidity?' "

You couldn't blame Dave's employers if they concluded he had a bit of an attitude problem. Occasionally he referred to his corporate overlords as the "Avco Broad-baiting Castoration," an appellation he found considerably more humorous than the execs of Avco did. Privately, he joked about the station's account execs as "sharks in sharkskin suits." When he attended the once-a-year meeting at which the president of the entire network came to Indianapolis to meet his far-flung employees, Dave feigned ignorance that the station's management had carefully orchestrated the question period, planting the questions they knew the president wanted discussed. He stood up and asked a real question about when some long-awaited minor improvement in the building was going to take place, causing consternation all the way round. And it wasn't only executives who found themselves the object of Dave's ironic attitude. One earnest young intern had the misfortune to believe Dave's explanation of the way he was supposed to erase a videotape for reuse. The young man sat for hours painstakingly going over the tape with the eraser of his pencil, while Dave chortled endlessly just out of earshot.

Even in those early years, Dave had his loyal fans, people who would stay up to watch *him*, if not the "freeze-dried movie." But as Dave himself was the first to admit, his on-the-air brand of humor was not to everyone's taste. Ron Pearson reinforces this point. Like Dave, he had gone to Indianapolis after graduation and eventually landed a position on Channel 13's sales team. As the youngest, and no doubt hippest, member of the team, he was the one elected to go out and find sponsors for Dave's shows. He recalls that some of the more progressive merchants in Broad Ripple were willing to sign up on a trial basis, out of loyalty to a neighborhood product and the hope that others in the area would feel the same way. But sooner or later the sponsors would get a chance actually to *watch* the program they were paying to keep on the air, and in many cases, their enthusiasm promptly waned. Somehow, it just wasn't what they had expected from big-time TV.

Dave was no doubt aware of the miasma of disapproval collecting over his head, but he was enjoying himself and he didn't want to take it all too seriously. He rather liked the little niche he had found for himself. He later explained, "I had no desire to be an anchorman, because in the early seventies, the idea was that the TV news should be as slick and straight as possible." As fans of *Late Night with David Letterman* know, "slick and straight" are anathema to Dave. So he continued to make fun of earnest 4-H youths and to deliver improbable weather forecasts. "I used to like to make up cities and circumstances that didn't exist and describe devastation that didn't occur. I thought that was a high form of entertainment. Looking back on it, it probably wasn't funny, but I enjoyed using television for the purpose of disseminating false data." And of course, he still does.

If the viewing masses had not yet discovered the fun of being with David Letterman, people who knew him personally had. He described his social life for *Playboy*. "I remember being surprised when I got out of college that the real world was unlike the fraternity house. . . . The people I was working with weren't drinking as much beer as I was. So I'd find the two or three guys who still were and they would be my friends. And we had plenty of fun being young adults loose on the town. We'd just go out every night after work and drink." Tom Cochrun, who had by this time also begun to work in Indianapolis broadcasting, says Dave was always amusing in social situations. He tells the story of a party at his house to which Dave was invited. It was a crowd of up-and-coming young Indianapolites and apparently Dave thought it needed a little watering down. Shortly after his arrival, he disappeared into the bathroom, wet his hair and slicked it down, stripped to his T-shirt, and rolled a pack of cigarettes in the sleeve; if he'd had time, no doubt he would have run out and gotten tattooed on the biceps. He was good enough in his assumed persona to baffle many of Tom's other guests.

Dave and Michelle themselves sometimes entertained.

Several friends remember that dinner at the Lettermans' was a pleasant experience, and Michelle a gracious hostess. And Dave liked to get together a few friends to go to the baseball game (Indianapolis has a AAA club, the Indians, that brings out strong local support). He was a knowledgeable and enthusiastic spectator—still is.

None of the above should be construed to mean that Dave had become just an ordinary guy. If clothes can be said to make the man, then God alone knows what Dave's clothes made him. He was often seen wearing scruffy old jeans, cutoff sweatshirts, and a very battered old sports-car cap. The beard he sported didn't help either; bushy and untrimmed, it was more collegiate than sophisticate. And his hair didn't seem to be any more successfully cut than it was in the old days. Dave's outfits might have made him a bit informally dressed among a group of construction workers; for a local television personality, he was definitely unconventional.

Other aspects of his life-style remained unconventional as well. He and Michelle had moved from their previous odd location to a new one, just as odd for a young couple—a big, old apartment building with almost no residents other than themselves under the age of seventy. Dave seemed to relish it, especially for the big metal electrical tower just outside the window. (He liked to call it "the nuclear reactor.") He was still biking to work, but decided to invest in another means of transportation and bought a canoe. Presumably its real purpose was for days in the country surrounding Indianapolis, but Dave liked to imagine using it in a more urban setting. One of the unusual features of Indianapolis is the presence of a canal that starts at a dam on the White River, very near Broad Ripple High School, and meanders across the city, through Butler University and Fall Creek Park, ending in the heart of downtown only a few blocks away from the state cap-

itol. Dave tried to interest Ron Pearson in coming along
with him, dressed in black clothes with charcoal on their
faces, to see if they could get all the way downtown in
his canoe without being detected. Eventually he gave up
the fantasy of commuting to work in a canoe and bought
a red pickup truck instead. Such trucks are of course
common vehicles in all the farming communities surrounding Indianapolis, but it seemed a somewhat exotic
choice for someone who used it principally to commute
to his job at the TV station at 14th Street and Meridian.
People who knew Dave in those days thought it was very
important to him not to "sell out" for the sake of success
in the broadcasting industry, and his wardrobe and other
possessions that often act as status symbols seemed deliberately selected to prove that no such character collapse
had occurred.

Of course, there was always the provocative question
of whether or not Dave would ever be offered the *tempation* to sell out. Was there a buyer? Did Indianapolis
television want his soul? Did it even want his body? You
can be sure Dave wasn't yearning for the chance to take
over as the regular weatherman. And he didn't hope to
make anchorman someday either, since he had always
observed that all he would then be allowed to do was
read what was on the TelePrompTer. Except for the news,
there wasn't much locally produced programming in the
Midwest. Shows like *Clover Power* and *Freeze-Dried Movies*
were probably about the best opportunity to use his own
material he'd ever get in Indianapolis. It's easy enough
to understand why the prospect of years toiling away on
such shows didn't exactly enchant him. Nor did he simply
want to settle for being a minor celebrity in a minor market. He later remarked astringently, "I could have become
one of any number of guys who have stayed on in any
market of the country. There are guys who have been on

twenty-five years; they become Fred Heckmans [a prominent broadcaster in Indiana], they become the dean of this and the dean of that, and they speak at the Rotary club and the next thing you know they're dead."

David Letterman was determined to avoid such a fate. The next step was obvious: he ought to try for a job on television in a larger market. He says he sent tapes of his on-the-air performances to many stations around the country several times every year, but it was clearly to no avail. "They would look at the tape, erase it and keep it in their files to record their weekend sports. I was losing a fortune in videotapes and I couldn't get a job because nobody wanted a smartass on the air."

After a while, it occurred to him that perhaps radio might offer him more opportunities than television. Radio, after all, requires a lot of local programming, with the various interview and call-in shows, some on special subjects and some of general interest. And a radio show usually gives the host several hours a day to be on the air, thereby making more of an impression on listeners than *Clover Power*'s half hour would permit. Radio waves even travel farther, thus expanding the size of one's potential audience.

One other big plus about radio was that no one could see you while you were doing it. Dave was (probably still is) basically a shy guy who found it difficult to get up and be funny while people were watching. He told *Playboy*, "As a kid I loved the image of Arthur Godfrey doing his radio-TV simulcasts, sitting behind a microphone wearing headphones—just talking. That was my fantasy: being able to communicate with folks without the unspeakable trauma of having them right there in the same room, scrutinizing me. Even later, when I did local radio and TV in Indianapolis, the thought of appearing live anywhere was just out of the question. People would say,

'Hey, Dave, the Kiwanis Club wants you to come over and kiss their children,' and I'd say, 'No, I can't do that.' "
Of course, at WLWI, his television appearances took place in a small studio guaranteed free of any live spectators, but there was always the unnerving thought that someone would actually see you on their set at home. How much nicer to be completely invisible, a disembodied voice floating on the radio waves, entering people's homes to do mischief.

Late in 1974, David Letterman left Channel 13 and went to work for Indianapolis radio station WNTS. The station was a well-meaning experiment with all-talk radio (it later switched to all religion and had much greater success) carrying some syndicated programs and some originated locally. For unknown reasons, WNTS had an unusually large number of interns working at the station, which gave it somewhat more of a team atmosphere than is usual at most such places. Dave was assigned the afternoon drive-time show, one of the prime-time slots, and took over as host of a call-in show.

Almost from the beginning, he realized he was not well suited to the job. As he told Debbie Paul, "I hated it. I was miscast because you have to have somebody who is fairly knowledgeable, fairly glib, possessing a natural interest in a number of topics. That certainly is not me: I don't care about politics; I don't care about the world economy; I don't care about Martians cleaning our teeth. The Nixon-Watergate nonsense was the perfect example of something about which I knew nothing and couldn't have cared less. All I wanted to do was get home at the end of the day and drink beer. In the meantime, all these political mavens would call wanting to discuss the intricacies of the left and the right and what did I know? I was just your average jerk, so I didn't do them much good. I did it for a year and literally thought I would lose my mind." He later lamented, "This was around the time of Watergate, and most of our callers thought homosexuals and people from Jupiter were behind it all."

By now, you can probably guess what David Letterman would do when faced with daily work he found boring and unrewarding. That's right; he started to make jokes out of things that other people took seriously. And his radio program gave him a lot more scope than he'd ever had at Channel 13. One of the things nearly everyone in Indianapolis remembers about Dave's stint at WNTS is that he told his listeners that their beloved 230-foot-tall Soldier's Monument (quite literally the focal point of the city, located in the circle in the middle of its hub) had been sold to the island of Guam, whose government planned to paint it green in honor of their national vegetable, the asparagus. In its place would be built a miniature golf course. Needless to say, a certain segment of his audience believed this bad news and began protesting vociferously. For Dave, it was all in a day's work. More false information being disseminated over the airwaves.

Another of Indianapolis's sacred cows is the Indy 500, and you can be sure the race came in for a fair share of jokes. For days before the big event, Dave started building up imaginary dissension among the competitors. Finally he announced that a "rump group" was breaking away to form their own association and hold a rival race. He claimed it was going to be held on Interstate 70, from Indianapolis to Kansas City, and warned motorists to look out for speeding racers. Muncie resident and "Garfield" cartoonist Jim Davis, another Ball State alum who knew Dave slightly during their college days, told *Rolling Stone* about some of Dave's other fictions in regard to sports. "He would announce fictional sporting events on the radio. In one sport, the ball was supposedly about eight feet in diameter, and the object was to get it out of the stadium and into the opposing team's bus. He would sit there and announce the darn thing on the air. Some people believed it."

It was while at WNTS that Dave began what has now become a venerable tradition on *Late Night*—teasing Jane Pauley. She had also grown up in Indianapolis, and went to Warren Central High School, in the district next to Broad Ripple. As she later had fun pointing out to Dave in public venues, she *did* get into Indiana University, and then she returned to Indianapolis to work in the newsroom at Channel 8. She was young, attractive, successful—a perfect target for Dave. (Sort of like those high school girls whose houses he used to egg based on his untested assumption they'd never agree to go out with him.) One of his most effective teases came the day he announced on his program that Jane Pauley was getting married that day and urged listeners to send her congratulatory cards and presents. It all came as a surprise to Jane, who actually had no marriage plans at the time. As *Late Night* fans know, Jane Pauley continues to be one of Dave's favorite objects of humor. And it's not just confined to the show either. Several years ago, Jane wrote a letter to the editor of the *Indianapolis Star* to protest the way a planned upgrading of the Broad Ripple High School would affect the immediate residential neighborhood (where her parents now live). Recognizing that David Letterman was Broad Ripple's most famous graduate, someone at the paper asked him for a letter that could be published at the same time as Jane's. Dave's letter was brief and to the point. "As a graduate of Broad Ripple High School and long-time neighbor, I take the position that whatever Jane Pauley says goes double for me."

Dave had other targets for his teasing as well. One of them was Indiana's then governor, Otis Bowen, later to hold a cabinet post in the Reagan administration. It struck

Dave as funny (disseminating more false information) to call him Governor "Bowman," and when people called in to correct him, he launched into long explanations of how the man's name was usually mispronounced "Bowen" through sheer carelessness. David was so convincing that people started calling the governor's office to find out what his name really was.

The show at WNTS may have been where Dave learned some of the comedic techniques that work so well on *Late Night*, especially his counterpunching style of interviewing. He customarily gave the folks calling in enough rope to make themselves look foolish, and then all he had to do was point it out, usually by affecting to take everything they said quite seriously. A lot of people thought it was hilarious. Lou Sherman, an Indianapolis radio personality who worked at WNTS during that time, remembers that most of Dave's colleagues admired his talent and thought he was funny. "He had the ability to take those things that are around us every day but we don't really notice and focus on them in a humorous way," said Lou. "We were not surprised that he later succeeded the way he did." Yet there are also those who remember listening to the show in stunned amazement. One Indianapolis resident said that he would cut callers off "something terrible." If he couldn't think of any way to make what the caller was saying work for him in a comic way, he would simply ditch the person abruptly. "This caller must be from Mars," he would conclude as he hung up. Then, instead of taking another call that might turn out to be as big a loss as the previous one, he would switch to doing some monologue of his own.

Dave used his program staff as an involuntary repertory company (an idea he still likes to play with on television, when he drags production assistants on the air to reveal some backstage secret to the audience). One of his young producers was turned into a character he called "Kitty Country." He talked about her taste in country music and her love affairs with cowboys—much to the embarrassment of the young Indianapolis woman who found herself thus transformed. Or he would call on a staff member without warning, with some threatening introduction like, "Here is Ted with Cool Guy tips," and then allow the poor man to flounder around for a time before he came to the rescue.

Another identifying characteristic of the *Late Night* David Letterman that can be traced to the days at WNTS is his use of silly little catch phrases derived from earlier, more innocent broadcasting days. Lou Sherman remembers hearing Dave address his audience as "you home listeners" and concluding various ads and announcements with the tag "You'll be glad you did." Ron Pearson remembers hearing, "In our society, as we know it today," and "Remember, you heard it here, folks." Ron believes these phrases were initially a way for Dave to buy a few seconds of time, during which he would "flip through his mental Rolodex" to come up with the right focus and wording for his next funny remark—the way musicians will vamp until they are ready to swing into the next number full tilt. Many stand-up comics do something of the sort with their fill-in phrases, such as "But seriously, folks," or reiterated themes such as "That's the kind of day it was." What is unusual about the way Dave does it is that even his fill-in phrases are funny and also serve to reinforce his comic perspective of the somewhat bemused boy from the country taking everything he hears too seriously.

Although certain aspects of the talk show radio format allowed Dave more time and freedom than he'd had on television, he was not really cut out to be the host of a call-in talk show. As the months went by, he liked it less and less, and friends remember it as a difficult period in his life. He concluded it was time for him to move on, and he'd already discovered he wasn't likely to get a better job at any midwestern radio or television station. His thoughts began to turn toward employment at the network level, and the niche he thought might be right for him was writing scripts for comedy shows. When he watched TV sit-coms or comedy specials, he used to say to friends, "I can write stuff that funny," and he was probably right. Of course, the problem he faced was to get producers to agree with him.

He considered going either to California or New York to search for a chance to use more of his talents—and have more fun doing it. He had some savings to help him over the transition. Although he probably never earned more than $20,000 a year in his Indianapolis broadcasting career, he and Michelle were a fairly frugal couple and he always handled his financial affairs conservatively. Dave was not the kind of guy who would just decide to go somewhere and wing it. He wanted to have his goals in mind and his financial arrangements solidly behind him. Tom Cochrun calls Dave a person who always wanted to have the situation mastered, with no surprises likely to spring up in his path.

Dave eventually chose Los Angeles over New York. He was helped in the momentous decision to head west by Michelle's enthusiasm. She was always his biggest fan and head cheerleader, and she was sure he would take L.A. by storm. "She started running around and packing the dishes and telling me this time we were really gonna do it. She was very supportive. I knew I was going to fail." Tom Cochrun remembers going on a picnic in southern Indiana a couple of days before the Lettermans left for the coast. Although Dave had agonized over making the decision to leave, once it was made he seemed relaxed and happy. He told Tom that he knew he could stay in Indianapolis and settle into a career as a local radio or TV personality, but he felt he wanted to try for something more.

Tom Cochrun agreed it was the right move. "Dave had a talent that was bigger than the city of Indianapolis."

Chapter

5

California Dreamin'

In a 1982 interview for *Success* magazine, David Letterman talked about the way he felt as he and Michelle drove out to California in the red pickup. "Ultimately, it wasn't so much a matter of bravery. You keep conditioning yourself in risk situations. 'Well, if it all explodes in my face, I can always come back to Indianapolis and get work.' So I convinced myself by looking at the other side of the argument that I really had nothing to lose. You sort of trick yourself into thinking that it's an extended vacation or a high adventure. But the truth of the matter was I felt pretty foolish giving up a job that was making good money for me. Driving across the country that May, I felt pretty stupid."

Things didn't improve much upon his arrival in Los Angeles. Here's what Dave later told a *Playboy* interviewer about those first few months. "I told everyone, including myself, that I was going out there to become a TV scriptwriter. I thought that would be my best entry point into the business. But the thing you discover is that you can write all the scripts you want when you're living in Indianapolis. People aren't going to meet you at the L.A. city line saying, 'Can we see those scripts? We're dying to get scripts from people who live in Indianapolis.' It just doesn't work that way. I'd take my scripts around and they'd toss them into a warehouse, and every Thursday, the guy with the forklift would go by, pick up all the scripts and bury them near the river."

In other words, moving to L.A. initially brought a good deal of discouragement. The world of television comedy was not eagerly awaiting his arrival but merely indifferent to his existence. Scripts that had seemed to him at home to be combustibly humorous failed to strike a single spark when exhibited in public. Even the few contacts he had hoped might lead to something were fruitless. For example, he had met Betty White and Allen Ludden when he worked at WNTS. The station carried one of their syndicated radio shows, and they sometimes came to town to do a little discreet promotion. They thought Dave was funny, and they didn't even object to being the butt of some of his jokes. Dave once told his listeners that Indianapolis's newest tourist attraction was going to be the Allen Ludden Wax Museum, and then urged them to honk if they wanted to cast their vote against this nasty turn of events. In L.A., Betty and Allen did what they could, which was to invite Dave to be a guest on their half-hour TV program called *What Is It?*, in which a panel is shown bizarre objects and asked to guess their purpose. It had all the earmarks of a good forum for any comedian, but the effect of Dave's appearance on his career was virtually negligible. Another disappointment came when Dave had his first meeting with the show biz agent to whom he had been referred. The man told him abruptly that he was quitting the business.

Dave is frank about the effect of those first few months in L.A. on his morale. "I panicked. It was the first time in my adult life that I didn't have a real job." The lack of a steady income worried this frugal Hoosier nearly as much as the lack of recognition it betokened. So there was a feeling of real relief around the Letterman household when Michelle landed a good job as a department-store buyer. With the threat of imminent poverty removed, Dave could concentrate on the question of how to create a career for himself in national television.

One obvious answer was to try his comedy material out in some public place. Everyone told him he should go to the Comedy Store, the most famous of all West Coast comedy clubs, on the night when the management turned the mike over to anyone who had the nerve—or stupidity—to climb up on the stage. The very thought of it made Dave anxious. He knew he lacked the experience: "I'd never performed as a stand-up comedian before, partly because there's just no place to do that in Indianapolis or Ball State. Oh, you can do it in your home, but it gets little response." He was sure he was funny, but he was by no means sure he was cut out to be a performer. Still, he understood that an appearance at the Comedy Store was like a demo tape sent to the right audience. It was where comics went and waited for lightning to strike. Dave explains, "Because the Comedy Store is there, people think, 'That's where I go to be a stand-up comic.' Look at the success of Steve Martin, who I think is very funny. He gets on stage in front of 10,000 people and acts like a jerk. It makes every kid who's ever goofed around in high school and made friends laugh think he might be able to do it."

So Dave took the risk. He labels his first night a terrible failure. "The first time, I found it very painful to get up in front of those people. And I wasn't exactly a big hit either. . . . I remember thinking, 'Jeez, I've come 2500 miles and gotten onstage in this dimly lit bar in front of these mutants, and I'm telling jokes.' " In a *Newsweek* interview, he characterized the problem: "I got up and said from rote some stuff I had written that day. Dead silence."

Although Dave remembers that first night at the Comedy Store as humiliating, not everyone agrees with him. Comedian Jay Leno was there, and he told journalist Bill Zehma that he was immediately impressed. "A lot of times on amateur nights, guys constantly do things like, 'What if Bob Dylan was a tree?' But all of a sudden, this new guy from the Midwest gets up and he has this really clever, hip material. He knocked everybody out. In fact, the only thing wrong with his act was that he had a big beard at the time. He looked like Dinty Moore."

Dave deftly returns Jay's compliments. The way he remembers it, his own comedy act didn't really take shape until he saw Jay's. "I thought, 'Aww, I see, *that's* how it's supposed to be done.' It wasn't two guys go into a bar, and it wasn't bathroom jokes. It was all smart, shrewd observations, and it could be anything—politics, television, education. The dynamic of it was, you and I both understand that this is stupid. We're Jay's hip friends." Later, Dave said in *Newsweek* about Jay. "His attitude was so clearly defined, and he was so bright and so contemporary and he did it so effortlessly, it just seemed like an extension of his personality. And that really crystallized for me what I wanted to do."

What Dave took from Jay Leno was a technique for getting his humor across and for weaving his singular observations into an extended piece of comedy. What he brought to it himself was his inimitable point of view, his way of looking at the ordinary and seeing the absurd. "I suppose I'm an observational comic. I try to serve my own sense of humor, and if other people like it, fine. What I look for are the setups in life, and then I fill in the punchlines. Like one of my favorite jokes came right out of the *National Enquirer*, which every week gives you a million setups. I'm standing there buying cantaloupes, and there's this headline in the *Enquirer* that says, 'How to Lose Weight Without Diet or Exercise.' So I think to myself, 'That leaves disease.' I've been doing that word for word for four years, and it never fails to get laughs. Or there was the time I was driving my pickup truck and I heard a guy on the radio screaming, 'Now you can buy breakfast at McDonald's.' And I thought, 'Boy, there's a dream come true.' They're not so much jokes as they are sarcastic comments, expressions of an attitude."

Some of his early comedy originated back in Indianapolis talk radio. For example, he told Comedy Store patrons the Indiana definition of a dope ring: "a group of Hoosiers standing in a circle holding hands." Most of this was soon replaced by less parochial jokes. As Dave polished his act, he moved from the ranks of amateurs to professional status. The Comedy Store engaged him as one of their regulars and actually paid him to tell jokes. But he never really relaxed into enjoying the act of live performance. "I envy comedians who can go out and enjoy being in front of people. It's still something of a traumatic thing for me," he told *TV Guide* some years later. "I'm generally uncomfortable around people. I'm also a confirmed pessimist—if anything can go wrong, it sure as hell will."

Pessimist's fears notwithstanding, nothing was going wrong with his career. In fact, his regular appearances had attracted the attention of comedian Jimmie Walker, at that time starring in the sit-com *Good Times* as the big-mouthed toothpick "J.J." Walker hired him as a joke-writer, with a weekly salary of $150 for fifteen jokes. "He wanted me to write jokes with a black point of view," explains Dave in a voice of sweet reason. "Which was interesting, because he was the first black person I had ever seen." He concludes, "Who better to capsulize the American black experience than a white guy from Indiana? But Jimmie was very, very nice." Dave thought he was also shrewd about his career planning. "He realized that he'd be able to sustain himself in show business long after *Good Times* was gone, through his stand-up act, so he hired punks out of the Midwest to keep building his material. . . . I'll always respect the way he thought about his career in the long view." Meanwhile, the money Jimmie Walker paid Dave was a big help to the family budget, and being paid to write jokes for a successful TV comedian helped to bolster his confidence. "I'll always be grateful to Jimmie for that early support."

Grateful as he was for the work, he was also determined to see that he didn't have the job for very long. "Writing comedy for someone else is not as rewarding as performing it yourself," he pronounced—bold talk for a man who is uncomfortable with a live audience of more than three people. He added, "There's not as much money in it. If I write a joke for you and you tell the joke for the rest of your life, I'm not getting any credit for it. You may have paid me $50 for it, but still and all, it's yours." So there were practical reasons for wanting to tell the jokes himself.

The hope of most people who work at the Comedy Store is being discovered by someone in TV—and I don't mean Jimmie Walker. For a number of years, the Johnny Carson show has used the Comedy Store almost like a farm club. People from the show go to the club regularly, and when they spot a likely new talent, an appearance on Carson's show is frequently the outcome. According to Dave, "The people at *The Tonight Show* are very good at dealing with young comedians. . . . They want nothing more than to break another Freddie Prinze, and they keep track of everybody." Among those who have moved from the Comedy Store to the Carson show to wider fame are Robin Williams and Andy Kaufman. The hope of adding his name to that group was one of the major reasons Dave had decided to give live performances a try.

Carson had been one of Letterman's heroes for years. He claims he used to watch Johnny back in the 1950s (when *The Tonight Show* was still being hosted by Steve Allen and Jack Paar) on a comic game show called *Who Do You Trust?* Dave says enthusiastically, "There was one guest who balanced a lawn mower on his chin—quite a booking coup—and Carson just made fun of him. I thought, 'What a great way to make a living!' "

Dave recounts, "In 1977, [the Carson people] came to me and said, 'You're not ready.' I said, 'OK, that's fine.' I was just thrilled they'd been watching me. And the last thing you want to do is go on and not be ready. So I kept working and building my act, and the next year, they called for me."

The reason talent scouts for *The Tonight Show* had finally arrived at that conclusion was that they had seen Dave on other television shows. Early in 1977, Dave was signed to a contract by the management firm of Rollins, Joffe, Morra & Brezner, a prestigious firm whose other clients include Robin Williams, Billy Crystal, and Woody Allen. They had spotted him at the Comedy Store and immediately recognized his potential. As Jack Rollins explains, "The format was hard to guess, but the medium wasn't. David has a readiness to have things bubble out of him. That's an enormous strength in television, where everything is quick and short." So his managers began knocking on doors, and Dave began getting jobs here and there. He did some miscellaneous comedy writing for show biz figures as diverse as Bob Hope, Paul Lynde, and John Denver. But he also began to get performing opportunities in TV. He did a stand-up routine on *The Gong Show* and a program called *Rock Concert*. Then he was offered a spot as a regular on a comedy called *The Peeping Times*, which was conceived as a parody of *60 Minutes*. It was a good opportunity, but it also brought Dave up against industry image-makers for the first time.

Let David tell the story. "The week before we started shooting I get a call from a secretary who says, 'We've been trying to get hold of your agent but we can't reach him, so we're just going to tell you—you've got to get your teeth fixed.' I run to the mirror thinking 'Teeth?' and honest to God I notice for the first time that I have these huge spaces between my teeth. I fought it but finally they said you can get inserts. [That's what model Lauren Hutton used to solve a similar problem.] Which was fine except that when I wore them, I couldn't speak properly— every P just exploded into the mike. So I'm not going to get my teeth fixed." And just so you remember that Dave Letterman doesn't sell out, "And I'm not going to get rid of my pickup truck because it's gotten to the point where it irritates people. You roll up to some place in Beverly Hills where they've got valet parking and they go, 'Oh, Christ, I ain't parking that. Guido, you park it.' "

It was probably just as well that Dave didn't make himself over to the specifications of *The Peeping Times*, because the show was extremely short-lived. Still, the exposure made it possible for his managers to get him a spot on a 1977 summer replacement show called *The Starland Vocal Band Show*. (Back in those days, they actually waited until the summer to replace a sagging show, instead of jerking it off the air the first moment its ratings dipped, as is now the custom.) The vocal group was of course the star of the show, but Dave got a few comic moments of his own.

On the strength of this growing list of television appearances, Rollins, Joffe succeeded in getting Dave a prominent spot on a show for which everyone had high hopes. It was a variety hour starring Mary Tyler Moore, the first thing she had agreed to do after her hit sit-com went off the air. The show was produced by MTM Productions, and a lot of television's heavy hitters were involved with it: Grant Tinker, for example, was the producer. Dave would do some of the writing, and he would also perform on the show.

At the same time that Dave was contemplating that exciting career opportunity, he was also dealing with a less happy aspect of reality. His marriage to Michelle had pretty much fallen apart. One reason was a scheduling difficulty. "My wife was working as a department-store buyer. So at night she would come home and I would go out. We started not seeing each other week in and week out. And that was the reason for the divorce, ultimately. We just didn't know who we were." He's adamant that his marriage was not a casualty of a show business career. "It could have happened in Indianapolis or Tucson. The marriage just ran out of steam."

Some of his most explicit public remarks about his and Michelle's problems were in that *Playboy* interview. "It was not," he said emphatically, "a case of my getting a taste of the fast life in show business and saying, 'To hell with this old broad.' " His conclusion was, "Our basic problem was that we'd just gotten married too young." Perhaps they'd also gotten married for some of the wrong reasons. Five years after the divorce, he described their marriage as "a common mistake. You're just looking to Take A Step Into Something to get away from being a kid." Neither of them had had a chance to learn who they really were before they merged into a couple, and they both wanted the opportunity to find out. So in 1977, they were divorced. The decision was not without its emotional cost. "I was really committed," he reflected, "and I couldn't believe it when it came to an end." It's not the way you are brought up back home in Indiana to think things will turn out; marriage is supposed to be forever.

Dave says he never intended getting involved in another relationship. But he met an interesting and talented woman at the Comedy Store who quickly became an important part of his life. Her name was Merrill Markoe. Like Dave, she was interested in writing and performing comedy. In most other ways, she was his total opposite. Or as David put it, "She's verbal and uncompromising about what's worth pursuing. She's intelligent. Nothing like I am." In fact, she was a graduate of the University of California at Berkeley and had been a bit of a campus radical. (How could you be a student at Berkeley without being radical?) After she graduated with a major in fine arts, she got a job teaching art at the University of Southern California. "I realized it was dull," she admits, "so I tried writing." She worked up a stand-up act of her own and appeared at the Comedy Store for much the same reason Dave did, to showcase her comedic talent. But in her case, she preferred the idea of writing jokes for someone else. When she and Dave began dating, they both realized they also made a good professional team.

It was actually a pure coincidence that led Merrill to a job as a writer for Mary Tyler Moore's variety show, but it was Dave's good luck because she was able to help him over some of the worst hurdles. His role on the show was that of a wisecracking announcer, a foil for Mary's "sweet girl" persona. Dave explains, "It was a 'what's wrong with this picture' thing: straight Mary and bent David—and her trying to get me to sing and dance, which made me retch." And he's not talking just about the character he played, but about David Letterman himself.

David Letterman is a comedian, but that doesn't mean he is willing to be a clown. It's important to him to preserve his dignity and his integrity when he appears in public, and he feared that his attempts to sing and dance were nothing more than humiliating. "I was just mortified," he recalled in the *Rolling Stone* interview. "I was like a spring that was coiling ever more tightly." Merrill added that she did her best to protect him from the worst of it by trying to make sure the writers selected some other performer for the most humiliating possibilities, such as dressing up as a carrot or a gopher. She explained her motivation for such acts of kindness: "Because later I'd have to go to dinner with David, and hear him say, 'I DON'T WANNA DO IT!' So I was just trying to keep dinner easygoing."

In a 1986 *Newsweek* article, David summed up his own attitude toward being on *Mary*. "It was pretty exciting, having heard about Television City all my life, to be going to work there. I had a name badge with a picture on it and an ID number, and I could eat in the CBS commissary. I could talk to Mary Tyler Moore anytime I wanted. I could do almost anything. I could share fruit with her if I wanted to. I, of course, wanted to. She never wanted any part of it. But the hard part was that I had to sing and dance and dress up in costumes. That was tough. I knew my limitations, but this really brought 'em home. You know, it was, 'You're not a singer. You're not a dancer. You're not an actor. Get out of here. What are you doing? Get away from Mary. That's her fruit. Don't try and eat that fruit.' "

Actually, David's colleagues were nowhere near as critical as this sketch of life with *Mary* implies. Mary enjoyed working with him, and Grant Tinker was quite complimentary. "I'm a big David Letterman fan. He makes me laugh. I first noticed back then that he was quite special."

However special David may have been on the show, the show itself apparently struck the viewing public as something less than a thrill. After a summer's worth of preparation, it was on the air for all of three weeks, from September 24 to October 8, 1978. Then CBS abruptly canceled it. Yet despite its short life, *Mary* proved to be a turning point of sorts for David Letterman. Johnny Carson's people, who had already seen him live at the Comedy Store and thought he wasn't "ready," saw him again on the little screen and decided he had ripened. At last Dave was ready. On November 26, 1978, he walked through that curtain and onto the stage of *The Tonight Show*.

It might almost be true that the rest is history. On his very first appearance, Johnny asked him to come over and sit down after his comedy routine was finished. This is a high accolade; most performers who get on the show are treated like the hired help, summoned out for their moment in the spotlight and then dispatched back to whatever darkness lies behind that curtain. Only *stars* are invited to grace the chair next to Johnny's and exchange a few remarks with him, since that proximity implies some sort of parity of status. As Dave was to discover, it also confers it. Being seen on the show and then sitting next to Johnny makes all America sit up and take notice of you. Best of all, the success of his appearance made the producers of *The Tonight Show* invite Dave back again. Being on the Carson show, says David, "was the most fun I ever had. There I was, holding my own with Johnny Carson. I knew then I could hit big league pitching."

Fellow comedian and friend Tom Dreesen remembers the impact of that first appearance. "When he walked through the curtain on *The Tonight Show* for the first time, I got chills. I knew he had found his home. He did the strongest first shot I had ever seen." Dave expressed his own sense of the momentousness of the occasion in an interview with syndicated columnist Kay Gardella. "It was like looking at a picture of George Washington on a dollar bill all your life and suddenly being in a bar next to him. He was great. Very hospitable and friendly. Still, knowing you're under his scrutiny. . . . Everybody looks to him for his reactions. Comics are sensitive about how he treats them. One I know was upset because Johnny failed to mention his name when he finished a routine. 'Do you think that means anything?' he asked me."

If Dave thought it was exciting being a guest on the show, he was soon to discover an even greater thrill, that of being a guest host. "It happened real quickly," Dave explained. "During the middle of the third show, producer Fred de Cordova came over and said, 'Have your people call me about hosting.' That was a real numbing experience, having that go through my mind while I was still sitting there pretending to be part of the show." Dave later cracked, "At the time I saw that as a huge mistake on their part, but now I recognize it as an incredible bit of cosmic synchronization."

In *Rolling Stone*, he talked about the effect of this additional exposure: "In California, I was literally living in a one-room apartment on stilts in Laurel Canyon, and I had hosted *The Tonight Show* a couple of times, and then I went away. When I got back to my house in Laurel Canyon, I had mail from people all over the country, and they had all sent clippings carrying the same wire release saying I would be the next Johnny Carson. I thought, 'Good Lord.' The week before, I was having trouble getting enough money to have the clutch in my truck replaced, and the next week I'm getting clippings saying

I'm the next Johnny Carson. It just made me laugh. It was like finding gold in your junk drawer. It's like you find this thing and have it analyzed and then, 'No kidding? *It's pure gold?*' And they say, 'Yes, it is. It's worth six million dollars. We don't know how it got there but it's yours.' "

In 1979, David Letterman jokingly told a crowd of students at the Ball State homecoming how he got the job as guest host. "It's a theme contest," he cracked. "The author of the theme with the most grammatical problems is the winner." Asked to describe a typical day as a guest host, he replied, "I get up around three, take some pills, drink plenty of whiskey. . . . No, seriously, I get up early and meet with the producers. At five-thirty, I go numb. It's a real kick and the most pressure I've ever felt."

Over the next few years, Dave guest-hosted the Carson show more than twenty times (at a fee of about $1,000 a shot, slightly more than twice what they paid him to be a guest). So perhaps it was only natural that the talk started about how he would be the next Johnny Carson. Dave always told the press that he thought it was unlikely he'd be selected. Part of that was perhaps modesty, but part of it was also a rising conviction that he didn't really want to step into Johnny Carson's shoes. In one interview, he explained that, "It's exciting to guest-host, but not as exciting as doing the show *with* Carson. As a stand-up comic, you want his stamp of approval. He's the best straight man in the business." Later, he confided, "One night I was sitting there in Carson's chair and I said to myself, 'Well, wait a minute. I am not doing anything different. I am just being Johnny Carson. I knew that to make my mark in the world I had to do more of what I wanted to do."

David was perhaps most candid about the situation in an interview with Kay Gardella. "The association for me with the show has been good. For comedians, it's a real stamp of approval, and it's reflected in the money you make on the outside. I like doing the show and the people are supportive, but I can never fully relax because it's not my own show. You're driving somebody else's car and wearing somebody else's underwear. Carson has made it everything there is, so the best you can hope for is to be compared favorably to him.'' And that's just what happened to Dave.

In fact, there genuinely were a number of resemblances. Both Johnny Carson and David Letterman exude a midwestern sort of decency and genuineness. They both came across as relaxed personalities devoid of the giant egos that generally accompany show business success. Johnny is smoother, suaver, more given to sexual innuendo; David is quirkier, more cerebral, and somehow more innocent. Both men are great reactors, skilled at revealing the humor within a guest's most casual remark. They both seem less comfortable telling jokes than they do laughing at something that is going on in the studio around them. They are both capable of some cruel teasing of guests while still keeping audiences seeing things from their points of view. And Johnny and Dave both have that most valuable personality characteristic of a comedian, instant likability.

David himself had given a lot of thought to what it was that made Johnny Carson so successful for such a long period of time.

"First of all, I think Carson is real smart. One thing that would indicate that is that in TV, which is such a fluctuating quixotic medium, there are only a couple of people who have been on as long as he has. Dick Clark is another one; he'll die on the air and they'll cover his funeral during a cutout on the *Twenty Million Dollar Pyramid*. I think it's a sign of real intelligence that you're able to take your personality and make it sustain like that. Secondarily, there's Carson's personality itself. He just gives the impression that he's in control. He's likable, he can be real funny, he can be serious and, because you know he's not going to misdirect you, you're willing to put up with almost anything as long as he's in charge. Part of his secret is that midwestern thing. I guess you don't expect a guy from that part of the country, someone who looks like you or me, to be clever or tricky. It's a different image than the stereotype America has of comics—guys in shiny suits telling jokes about their wives' being fat. A Catskills comic can deliver a barb that leaves dead and wounded all around him, while a guy from Nebraska or Indiana can do it and it's a clean cut."

Many viewers, critics and audiences alike, had noticed similarities between the king of late-night television and the new phenomenon from the Midwest, David Letterman. So his name often led the list when there was talk about who would eventually replace Johnny. Smart money said David Brenner was too ethnic, Tom Snyder too weird, Joan Rivers too acerbic and obsessed with sex, Richard Dawson too much the buffoon. David Letterman alone seemed to meet all the imaginary requirements. As Johnny's producer, Fred de Cordova, put it, "David comes from the Midwest, the white bread section of the country."

For reasons of their own, NBC execs and people connected with *The Tonight Show* tacitly encouraged the speculation. It was good publicity: it made viewers want not only to watch Johnny to see what they might be missing, but also to tune in for each guest host to make their own judgment about his or her potential candidacy. The question of who was going to replace Johnny Carson began to seem like the search for the perfect Scarlett O'Hara, except that this time we all got to see the auditions. And of course, such speculation was a way to send a message indirectly to Johnny that perhaps despite the fact that 15.5 million people watched him every night and his show alone accounted for nearly 17 percent of NBC's pretax profits, he *was* replaceable; it might insure that his mutters of dissatisfaction didn't increase in volume. So all hands did what they could to incite the speculation without ever actually giving any candidate the inside track.

Fred Silverman, then the head of NBC, announced that "David is up there at the top of the list." Fred praised him for his "brilliant reaction," just like Carson's and said, "I think David has a very promising future with NBC." He refused, however, to say whether that future would be with *The Tonight Show* and made a point of commenting that there were at least five other good candidates for the position. David riposted, "I happen to know Fred Silverman doesn't even speak English, so what the hell does he know?" Fred de Cordova, Johnny's producer, made a statement that was so tactful it was positively uninformative. "David is extremely talented," he opined. "I think audiences identify with him and—this is not damning with faint praise—I believe he's getting better each time he does the show. And he was very good to start with. Everybody who has hosted the show is a candidate, although we hope Johnny stays on forever. I think he's irreplaceable, but I'm sure they said the same thing about Jack Paar when he left. I think David has a number of important qualities for hosting our show. He's charming and disarming, and we're always delighted when he's available."

Meanwhile, David did what he could to dampen the speculation, which definitely made him nervous. "I don't even think Carson is leaving," he said as if wishing could make it so. "If he does, I think he'll take the show with him to another network. I wouldn't want to go up against him—or compete with his seventeen-year legend. I'm just not eager to do it." In another interview, his sense of anxiety was somewhat more pronounced. "I had the feeling when I first guest-hosted that absolutely everything I was doing was being closely scrutinized. Eventually, I arrived at the stage where I decided I would just relax and enjoy myself. After all, it's flattering that I'm even in a position to be considered for the job." It sounds like the kind of determinedly optimistic attitude one is forced to adopt at 3 a.m. when the anxiety level gets too high and the need to get back to sleep is virtually overwhelming. Remember, this is a man who by his own admission always expects that Murphy's law will prevail and everything that *can* go wrong will. Replacing Johnny Carson could be the biggest break Dave could hope for, guaranteeing not only a nightly showcase for his own brand of humor but also wealth and fame for a lifetime. On the other hand, it could also be a booby trap, either destroying his career because of his perceived inability to fill his predecessor's shoes or destroying his spirit by locking him into a format and persona that were developed to fit someone else.

Dave's solution was to do his best to behave as if the possibility didn't exist—and after all, it was to a large extent a media hype rather than a genuine opportunity—at least for the moment. Johnny Carson was still in his chair every night (despite the jokes about the frequency of guest-host substitution), and Dave still had no "regular job" or fixed income. He confessed to one journalist that he thought that "a TV special bearing my name right now would draw about as much as a bucket of hot mud." So he took every guest shot he was offered, not only on the Carson show but other vehicles as well. He joked it up on *Hollywood Squares* and actually opened for Lola Falana at a hotel in Vegas—hard to believe, isn't it, folks? And he continued to appear at the Comedy Store, honing his act and trying out new comedic ideas. In his own humorous biographical sketch, Dave says of this period: "As a comedian, Mr. Letterman has performed on all the major talk and variety shows in Canada, and would be a major star in that country were it not for his frequent and vicious denouncements of Canada, its people, its weather and its bacon."

Alert viewers might have caught David Letterman even on game shows. For example, he appeared as a panelist on *The Gong Show*, sitting (with gong in hand) right next to Jaye P. Morgan. In 1979, he was a celebrity contestant for an entire week on *The Twenty Thousand Dollar Pyramid*, hosted by Dick Clark. Dave and fellow celebrity guest Joanne Worley both gave clues to and received them from their contestant partners, who stood to win that $20,000 if they could guess the words or categories that their partners were driving at. Dave looked like a typical preppy, wearing a tweed jacket, striped rep tie, and—so it appears—a pair of jeans. Compared to Joanne, he was a novice on the game-show circuit, and it showed. He looked awkward and ill at ease, and during the time he and his partner were actually competing, his face was often screwed up in painful concentration. He was slow and stiff in giving clues, but better at receiving them and guessing the correct answer. (His partners seemed to catch on to that, and when they went for the big money, they chose to give the clues themselves.) Only rarely did Dave manage to get off a joke of any sort, although as the week wore on he began to look a bit more relaxed. Still, it's interesting to see that Joanne Worley not only stole the show from him, she also was obviously considered by the studio audience to be a much bigger celebrity.

A little known fact about Dave's career during this period is that he actually worked as an actor. Well, maybe we should rephrase that: he was employed as an actor; whether or not he acted is a subject for debate. These moments of infamy took place on *Mork and Mindy*, and David Letterman had a small part in one of the 1979 episodes. Those who saw his performance (very likely to be a once-in-a-lifetime occurrence) say that he seemed awkward and ill at ease, and even those who love Dave most dearly, freely admit that he is no great shakes as an actor. Jay Leno, for example, calls him up every time some bit on *Late Night* calls for a tiny bit of acting and congratulates him sardonically on his skill. "The funniest thing in the world is when I see David 'act' on his show. He'll do a bit and say something like, 'All right, put the gun down.' I get hysterical! I call him up and say, '*Wonderful* acting job.' " It seems that this appearance as an actor on Robin Williams's show is a part of Dave's career that he would like to forget, since he absolutely never refers to it. In fact, he has more than once announced that he has never done any acting and never will. Considering the way he performed on *Mork and Mindy*, he may well be telling the truth.

He found himself worrying about the rate at which television consumed his material. In a 1979 interview, he fretted, "Working as a stand-up has been occupying my mind for four years, and it took me that long to accumulate twenty-five or thirty minutes of material I felt comfortable with, that I knew would work. In two or three months, I had used all that on TV." He concluded, "The luxury of time is gone," and then tried to see the bright side of it. "Sometimes you can hit gold writing jokes to a deadline. I'm certainly more productive than I was when I had time to polish material." He still wasn't all that comfortable in front of a live audience, but he wanted to improve his performing skills. And with Merrill in his life, he had an additional source of material—and encouragement. She later cracked, "When I first fell in love with Dave, I was busy writing him jokes. It was like the things girls do for their boyfriends. You know, 'Well, here. Take all these. Here are my best jokes.' "

There were surely times when he felt discouraged. His guest appearances were often on trivial shows, and he was acutely aware that as a celebrity, he was less than top-ranked. He told *Playboy* later how he had appeared on *The Liar's Club* as a "celebrity" and called that fact a "source of amusement." And he recognized that appearing in comedy clubs had to be temporary. He commented, "Unfortunately, people generally tend to stay too long at the Comedy Store and the Improv. They keep thinking, 'Maybe next week Merv Griffin will come in and put me on *Dance Fever*.' So they stay and stagnate and eventually come to be looked upon by the talent scouts as somehow tarnished. You know, who wants a guy who's been in junior high for eight years? Those clubs are a stepping stone. They're not a career."

A measure of his self-doubt was his failure to go back home to Indianapolis for some time. "I didn't go home for nearly four years. I felt embarrassed because I had not accomplished anything, plus I had just gotten a divorce—it was awkward to come home."

But in the eyes of the home folks, Dave *was* a celebrity. Family and friends kept track of his every television appearance, and his small but loyal cult-following from his years in Indianapolis broadcasting still wanted to hear from him. Lou Sherman remembers that one of the WNTS talk-show hosts, Bill Crofton, used to call Dave in L.A. on his morning show—which of course made it still the middle of the night in California. He'd interview Dave about his latest successes, and Dave would rise valiantly, albeit groggily, to the occasion with a barrage of jokes.

And when Dave returned to Ball State in 1979, to

appear in the show that celebrated Homecoming, he was treated like a full-fledged celebrity. Student reporters asked his opinion about everything from how to succeed in show business to how to pass mass communication, and then they wrote down his answers as carefully as if they had been inscribed on gold tablets. Everywhere he went, a crowd gathered. Merrill, who went with him, commented only half in jest, "Now I know what it would be like to have been married to one of the Beatles."

Another sign that Indiana considered Dave a real celebrity was that old buddy Ron Pearson, by this time a partner in an ad agency, asked him to appear in local commercials. Ron remembers he was able to offer Dave only a shamefully low fee for this work, but Dave threw himself into each project wholeheartedly. Standing on location at various Indianapolis merchants' places of business, Dave would ad-lib his own script. He might, for example, come up with bizarre "offers" for those who would come out and buy: a free haircut, perhaps, or free chili (but you had to bring your own bowl) or a free second opinion on the medical problem of your choice. Ron remembers one commercial in which Dave started out genially, "You're probably asking yourself what a major Hollywood star like me has in his house. Of course, there's the life-size cottage cheese statue of Debbie Boone. . . ." With that lead-in, it's hard to imagine that anyone could remember what Dave was actually selling. Ron says the tough part of doing a commercial spot with Dave was that his ironic quality always came through. If he tried to read ad copy straight, it sounded like he was making fun of it, so they were better off letting him do comedy from the very beginning; at least the audience would be laughing at the jokes, not the product.

Looking back on the big risk years later, Dave weighed the pluses and minuses and concluded that throwing up his job at WNTS in Indianapolis and going to California to try his luck didn't seem so foolhardy after all. "There really was no risk in my case. It was an imaginary risk. I always wondered why I couldn't get out of the city. I wondered why I couldn't get another job. And then when I just left and found myself succeeding by the definition of my peers, then I realized that, Jeez, if you want to do something, then you can certainly do it by just going to work on it. That was a real revelation for me." It was soon to stand him in good stead in the face of show biz adversity.

Chapter

6

A Show of
One's Own

The next turn of events happened swiftly. In the spring of 1979, Johnny Carson announced that he intended to escape from his NBC contract and retire on September 30. He admitted he had signed an agreement in 1972 that locked him into *The Tonight Show* until April, 1981. But he challenged the validity of the contract under a California law that prohibits personal service contracts that run for more than seven years. NBC, for its part, proclaimed that the existing contract was legally valid and that they expected Johnny to do his duty until it expired in 1981. Soon, both sides agreed that the matter should have a hearing in court. Behind the scenes, they continued to negotiate in the hope of a peaceful settlement.

It was within this context that NBC, in April, 1979, offered David Letterman an attractive two-year contract. No specific show was mentioned; NBC's goal was simply to get Dave on retainer while they waited to see what they would do with him. It doesn't take an Einstein to see that they wanted him in reserve in case negotiations with Johnny Carson didn't work out. By signing him to a contract, they insured that they had a substitute waiting on the bench; moreover, they served notice to Johnny that they were ready to get along without him—if they had to.

The best guess has it that the price for keeping Dave under exclusive contract was about $350,000 a year. And there was even an option for a third year, at NBC's discretion. It was enough money to make an ordinary guy from Indiana nervous. He told a reporter, "I keep waiting for someone to tap me on the shoulder and say, 'Okay, buddy, give us the money back, NBC wants your new house, and you have to go home to Indianapolis.' " He did, in fact, buy a new house, a lovely glass and redwood oceanfront place just north of Malibu, that he and Merrill considered home. But he didn't go so far as to trade in his pickup truck—a new set of tires was about all he was ready to spring for.

No doubt he was also nervous about waiting to hear what he would be expected to do to earn that money, because as the weeks passed, it looked more and more likely that Carson and NBC would settle their differences, leaving no opening for a Carson replacement. Where did that leave Dave?

Apparently, it left him as the star of a show called *Leave It to Dave*. Dave sums it up: "The whole project was just a disaster from word one." He wanted to do a goofy, off-the-wall kind of show (pretty much like the one he has now), but NBC experts said that would never work in the afternoon time slot for which the show was slated. It had to be an "afternoon show," they explained. So Dave waited to find out what that meant.

He learned all too soon. "I was supposed to sit on a throne, and the set was all pyramids. The walls were all covered in shag carpet. It was like some odd Egyptian theme sale at Carpeteria." Some of the plans for *Leave It*

To Dave began to make the experience of dressing up like a vegetable on *Mary* look good. "At one point I was in New York and I got a phone call from the West Coast. They said, 'We've come up with a great idea. Your guests will all sit around on pillows.' And I hung up the phone and I turned to my manager, Jack Rollins, and I said, 'This moron wants us to sit on pillows. What's the matter with chairs?' You could just see the elements kind of—I hate to say it was like dominoes toppling, but it was like dominoes toppling."

But that still left him with nothing to do. Johnny announced that he would continue with the show while the contract dispute ground its way through the courts, and soon all the talk about who would replace him died away. (He eventually signed another, more lucrative contract.) Dave's published remarks indicated that he was no longer very interested in live appearances at the Comedy Store or other clubs. "I don't want to spend my whole life working nightclubs before a bunch of drunks," he said flatly.

The NBC contract reportedly specified that Dave was guaranteed a late-night talk show pilot, a one-hour prime-time special, and a sit-com to write and develop—although not necessarily appear in, which suited him just fine. Dave joked that his favorite provision of the contract was that it gave him the right to live with Jane Pauley a few weeks out of the year. Dave and Merrill decided to begin work on the sit-com and told a reporter about its trailblazing qualities: "It won't have women with big busts, a black kid, a Chicano kid and a next-door neighbor."

As of this writing, we still don't know what kind of a sit-com those two fertile minds would have created, because before they could finish that project, David Letterman was tapped for another chance at stardom. He was given a talk show of his own. It was the answer to his prayers, except that, as we know, prayers are often answered in unexpected ways. The catch to this particular miracle was that the show would be on in the middle of the morning, at 10 a.m. As Dave later put it, "It was a strange land in which we found ourselves."

The driving force behind this turn of events was NBC head Fred Silverman. According to Dave, Fred told him that he could be the new version of Arthur Godfrey, a friendly folksy presence on the airwaves. It's interesting to learn from Dick Cavett's autobiography that he says Fred Silverman told him *he* could be the new Arthur Godfrey. We can certainly conclude that Fred was a man in search of Arthur Godfrey, and possibly not too particular about where he found him!

NBC laid down certain ground rules for the show. Implicit in the choice of a time slot was the assumption that it would appeal to housewives and have a "family feeling." As an innovation, it was decided to do the show live—and from New York.

Dave and Merrill left their Malibu house and looked for something to rent in New York. They first found an apartment at 55th Street and Sixth Avenue, an easy walk away from NBC's studios. The only problem was that, according to Dave, they lived "right where General Motors does their diesel equipment testing." As soon as possible, they moved to a quieter location on Manhattan's East Side. "We have a housekeeper and others who work on it when I'm not there. I don't know any of them, and they don't know each other, but I find little notes they send to each other about my life. I have a whole other life going on independently of me that I know nothing about." Working in Studio 6A in the RCA building, Dave was cautious about the move to the Big Apple. "I can't yet say I love New York, but we're still dating."

As to the format of the show, NBC pretty much decided to leave it to Dave. His first step was to hire Merrill as his head writer. Then he chose a producer, acquaintance Bob Stewart. Stewart was an experienced pro, but there was just one little hitch. His experience was all in the area of game shows rather than talk shows. In fact, he had been the director of *The Twenty Thousand Dollar Pyramid* when Dave had appeared on it as a celebrity contestant the previous year. Stewart's ideas for the program were strictly traditional. Celebrity guests, as many as could be booked; a little comedy material from Dave; and the occasional service-oriented segment, such as a fashion show, a "problem oriented" discussion or, as Fred Silverman suggested, a cooking demonstration. Just like Dinah Shore. . . . Meanwhile the advertising blitz began. "A face every mother could love!" the slogan went.

As the date for the debut of the show got closer and closer, Dave's disagreements with this type of program grew more and more obvious. Finally, four days before the show went on the air, Stewart left the program, at Dave's request. Dave later lamented to *Newsweek*, "Every day was a fistfight. The first director was a game-show director, and he could direct a game show in his sleep, but he couldn't direct a talk show. Basic rules of television directing were being violated left and right. . . . The guest would be saying something and the shot would be on me. I'd be talking, and the shot would be on who knows what. Finally, he started to shoot everything with one wide shot. It looked like a security camera at 7-Eleven."

News of Stewart's departure was reported very negatively in the press. For example, the *New York Post*'s gossip column, "Page Six," ran a long item that began, "In an astonishing high-level shake-up, the top two producers of the *David Letterman Show* have resigned—only days before this morning's scheduled debut of the NBC talk show. Producer Bob Stewart and associate producer

Anne Marie Schmidt left after reportedly losing a power struggle with comedian Letterman. . . . Letterman's daily ninety-minute live program is a pet project of his mentor Fred Silverman. The shake-up seems to indicate yet more trouble in the NBC studios—as well as Letterman's clout. Nobody will say what caused the turmoil, but insiders believe it had to do with format." Fred Silverman tried to quell the rumors. "It is going to capture audiences where tired game shows couldn't."

Merrill gamely agreed to step into the vacant spot and try to contain the crisis. David confessed, "The show was running us. Actually, it was chasing us down the street. But NBC told us not to worry. They said, 'You have twenty-six weeks; let it evolve.' "

The way the show evolved was based on recognizing that it is extremely difficult to go on the air and be funny for ninety consecutive minutes. Even people with a lot more broadcasting experience than Dave (and a lot bigger writing staff) find this virtually impossible. And Dave remembered from his guest-hosting on Carson's show how regular appearances can eat up comedy material. Even if he and Merrill could start out with a backlog of ideas, they'd probably use them all up in two weeks and be faced with the dilemma of creating more, at an ever faster rate. So to pace themselves, and to keep the show low-key, the way most experts agreed was necessary in the morning, Dave and Merrill decided to add a few other elements.

Okay, there would be a few celebrity guests. And in addition to David Letterman, there would be a cast of young comics to play takeoffs on traditional talk show guests. Edie McClurg, for example, played a household hinter called Mrs. Marv Mendenhall, and her tips came straight from Dave and Merrill. "How do you freshen up a room that's gone stale from too much air freshener?"

she asks rhetorically. "Old fish and garlic are good . . . also burnt cauliflower." Valri Bromfield played a rather dazed teenager named Debbie who was trying to get herself together; the effort encompassed such things as a trip to Kenya, where Debbie was shocked to discover that everyone was wearing their hair in corn rows just like Bo Derek. Paul Raley played P. J. Rails, a former FBI agent, who explained that his old boss J. Edgar Hoover was communicating with him from the beyond, through the medium of Helen Reddy's lyrics. He also expounded his conspiracy theories, in a long-running gag that placed Joe Garagiola (in full catcher's regalia) at the site of every major disaster of the twentieth century. Bob Sarlatte was the other member of this comedy family, and his mission was usually to banter with Dave.

Another regular feature was a couple of five-minute newscasts delivered by Edwin Newman. This public-service aspect of the program turned out to have an odd effect on viewers. As Newman sat at a desk in the studio and read the world news, studio audiences cheered and booed his reports. Apparently, the whole thing reminded them of *Saturday Night Live*'s "News Updates," and they took Newman's reports on, say, test-tube babies, as one more eruption of the comic spirit. Dave's initial intention was to have some other once-a-week regulars, such as columnist Jimmy Breslin, Senator William Proxmire reporting from Washington, the writer of a syndicated column about soap operas, and (much needed by this time) a psychotherapist. But as the show developed, most of these features were dropped. David tried to describe the show to previewing journalists. "It's my show, but one person can't fill it up. I think people will watch it for its elements. What will prevail is my attitude—not necessarily my on-camera attitude. And my attitude is pretty much that nothing should be taken all that seriously."

.The first show was broadcast on June 23, 1980. It had some distinctive Letterman touches. He came out and introduced himself as a man who had been a former guest host on the Johnny Carson show and then cracked, "But let's face it—who hasn't?" Instead of opening with a comedy monologue, Dave went out into the studio audience and began to chat. The upshot was that he sent one man visiting from Texas out to get coffee for other thirsty audience members (and tipped him when he returned). He went on to let his fans in on his favorite restaurant trick: "Ask the waiter for more parsley." Midway through the program, television critic Jeff Greenfield was brought on to review the show on the air. Bizarrely, much of the review concentrated on the inadequacies of the decor in the Green Room.

Most of the reviews of the first few installments of the *David Letterman Show* were not too warm. Headlines tell the story: "David Off to a Slow Start," for example, or "Letterman Live Just Lies There." Criticism tended to focus on the format of the show; David personally got good notices. Sad to say, the ratings were even worse than the reviews. The initial show won a rating of 1.4 and an 11 percent share of the audience. That put it squarely in last place among the networks, even against such flabby competition as reruns of *Laverne and Shirley* or *The Jeffersons* and *The Price Is Right*. In many markets, including New York, Dave's show even finished below some of the independent channels. Some people wondered aloud whether Fred Silverman had made a mistake in replacing *Hollywood Squares*, *High Rollers*, and *Chain Reaction* with nothing stronger than David Letterman.

David was immediately aware that the show was in trouble. "In the first week," he recalls, "you could hear the affiliates mailing in their cancellations." Although 170 stations out of a total of 212 NBC affiliates had agreed to carry the program, cancellations did begin as soon as the discouraging early ratings were in. "We had no problem with NBC till Boston announced that they were dropping out," David told the *New York Times*. "Then it was like a wave. Philadelphia, Detroit, and San Francisco went. The other shoe had dropped. We lost two dozen cities in a matter of weeks." In August, he admitted, "The first few weeks were very difficult. It was the real low point of my life, an awful period. Merrill and I'd sit around saying, 'Now, what do we do tomorrow?' " One of his answers was to feature on the show a "Cancellation Sweepstakes," in which he would invite viewers to guess the exact date on which the show would be canceled.

In this crisis, David discovered that NBC was less than wholly supportive. "We had a meeting with the NBC executive in charge of the show and she said, 'Well, you've just got to work harder,' and then she left for a four-day weekend in Maine. And I was screaming, 'What do you mean, *work harder*? It's like we've been holding back here? Like we know we've got a spot in the playoffs and now we'll really turn it on?' "

In fact, a good part of the problem was that Dave was working *too* hard. What he needed was a professional producer to shoulder some of the load. He credits Merrill for her brave effort: "She did a great job of holding things together, but through naïveté and inexperience, we made plenty of mistakes." And both were working such long hours that the tiredness sometimes showed on the air. They were so busy that the only time they could find to walk their dogs was in the wee hours of the morning. Merrill later recalled, "The morning show was a delusion in the sense that we felt you could just do whatever comedy you wanted, any time of day or night. And when the show started to fail, Dave was going crazy. It was not a happy time."

Things began to look up when a producer was finally found. He was Barry Sand, who had previously worked with David Frost, Mike Douglas, and *SCTV*. Barry remembers his first days on the job vividly: "Taking over the show was like going into the Normandy invasion in the first wave and not really knowing what you have to do." But at least one part of Sand's mission was crystal clear: he had to take some of the burden off David's shoulders and keep him relaxed enough to function at his best as a performer. "David and Merrill were doing everything," Sand explained. "There was no time for them to catch their breath and relax. Now David is listening more in the interviews. He has more confidence in the guests we have on the show and in the show's preparation. He is more comfortable and the show looks a lot better. The show we had was extremely cluttered, but now we have cleaned it up so that we can focus on the guy who is the star: David. If this show flops, it will have nothing to do with David Letterman." Sand also streamlined and improved the set; one critic said the original set "looked as if it had been thrown together by a drunk on a shopping spree at Azuma." And he hired director Hal Gurnee who gave the show its sense of pace.

Another decision made about that same time was also helpful, and that was to cut the show back to sixty minutes. That reduced the demand on the hard-driven staff for material, and it made it easier to pace the show; it became tighter and funnier. The repertory company idea completely disappeared as the show retrenched to concentrate on its strength—the wit and viewpoint of David Letterman. Johnny Carson, who had fought for years to get his own show cut back to a more manageable sixty minutes, sent David a telegram when he heard the news: "It took you two months to do what it took me seventeen years to do."

The network tried to help. They suggested more celebrity guests, which David didn't want to do, and more service segments such as tips on cooking and sewing, which David *certainly* didn't want to do. He later commented, "We got so much static from above, it became too hard to fight for what we believed in." Fred Silverman still believed in Arthur Godfrey and kept urging that the show be changed to move in that direction.

However misguided the advice from NBC, you can sympathize with their desire to do *something* about the show. Affiliates were still dropping like flies. David recollects, "There was a piece in the *Los Angeles Times* about the disaster that was daytime television, and it mentioned that the Westinghouse stations had pulled out and the affiliates were grumbling. That's how I found out about it." He tried valiantly to stem the tide himself by personally making calls to the station managers, asking them to hold on just a little longer. "I'd get on the phone to a guy in Buffalo, and he'd say, 'I think the show is great, but I'm looking at the figures here and *The Jeffersons* reruns are getting a 54 share against you. What am I supposed to do?' " Program director David Nelson of NBC affiliate KYW-TV in Philadelphia was typical. He told a *New York Times* reporter, "The *David Letterman Show* is well booked, well produced and nicely paced. David is witty, sharp, vulnerable, a sensitive communicator—all the things a talk show host should be." But Nelson dropped the program anyway. "There was nothing wrong with the show, except that it wasn't a morning show. Everything we knew about the morning says, 'Don't be too sharp, too fast-paced, too subtle.' People's batteries just aren't that charged up yet."

Oddly enough, in this discouraging situation, David's own spirits began to rise. He commented, "Every day, while we were struggling to put the show together, there'd be a story in the paper foretelling our doom. It eventually got to be fun. We created a kind of bunker mentality, trying to do as many unusual things as possible before the end came." In a way, it was like being back with the *Freeze-Dried Movies* on Channel 13 in Indianapolis. If no one was watching, and the show was going to be canceled no matter what anyone could do, why not have fun, please himself, do what he wanted to? That's when the *David Letterman Show* started to be really wonderful.

There are so many highlights of those last few weeks that it is hard to recapitulate them all. One was Floyd Stiles Day, held in honor of a retired Iowa janitor. Or how about the announcement of the opening of the Willard Scott Weather Museum in the basement of NBC? David claimed it included a photograph of the first cloud Willard ever saw. There was the time he produced some-one he claimed was the "psychological consultant" to the Democratic Party, and asked members of the audience to take ink-blot tests that supposedly could predict their vot-ing tendencies. As the audience members complied, Dave and the expert held a whispered consultation that resulted in two men in white coats coming to take innocent au-dience members away.

There was the time he worried that his viewers might be missing a program they'd like better, so he hauled out a television set and began flipping through the channels for their benefit. "There's an *Alice* rerun on Channel 2. . . . I think they found something in Mel's stew. . . . The Lone Ranger's on 5. . . . Uh, oh, here's Dinah cooking an omelet. . . ." After one commercial break, he came back saying, "I'm David Letterman, and I know my hair makes me look like a duck." Another time, he returned to tell his viewers that they had just missed the appear-ance of New York's mayor, Ed Koch—in the nude. When Pat Paulsen was on as a guest, Pat claimed he was going to levitate before the studio audience but warned, "I can't have people laughing." David shot back, "That hasn't been a problem so far." He pioneered some of the special events that still delight viewers on *Late Night*, such as volunteering to make the phone call that someone in the audience dreaded having to make, or asking people to bring in their cats and dogs for Stupid Pet tricks. One planned segment (never produced) would take members of the studio audience and send them down the hall, cameras following, to Fred Silverman's office. "I want them to meet the man who has given us *Sheriff Lobo* and *My Sister the Tuba*."

One of the wildest moments of the show came when David and the staff decided to throw a fortieth anniversary party for some couple they'd never seen before. Dave explained, "The party was great. The couple had invited all their friends, and it was catered and decorated. A band was playing. People were dancing. And while the couple were cutting the cake, we were dropping tulip petals on the entire aggregation." But it didn't all go smoothly for the happy couple. "We also had these giant sparklers going, and the sparklers began to ignite the flower petals. So all of a sudden, everybody was standing around in these little pockets of flame. And then a stagehand came out with a fire extinguisher, and that just made the fire spread. Plus, the studio audience suddenly thought they were about to become charred remains, and all of this was going out over the air. In the end, of course, no one was hurt. But phrases like 'ill-fated' were constantly being used to describe the morning show, and I don't think that's ever a good sign."

David also began to do more and more segments outside the confines of Studio 6A. Merrill told *Rolling Stone*, "On the morning show, Dave always wanted to go outside the studio. And it started out pretty easy. I had a big backlog of stuff that went by either geography or theme. We'd go down to Chinatown and tie everything together that I could write a joke into, or else we'd take a tour. One time we went to everything that had the sign WORLD'S BEST COFFEE." Another time they did a special report on vending machines at NBC, taking the mini-cam out into the hallways to see what it was possible to buy with the change in your pants pocket. It was what we would eventually come to recognize as vintage David Letterman.

The odd quality of those last weeks on the air was described by Barry Sand. "We were getting more and more absurd, and better and better—and going down in flames." David's own description was more graphic. "Every day I felt like I was in Vietnam." He also claimed that concerned fans were shouting at the referee, "Stop the fight! He's out on his feet!" In another interview he joked, "I was watching some program on TV last night and they said that by the late sixties, Mick Jagger and The Rolling Stones were known as the greatest rock and roll band in the world. I wish I could be introduced like that. You know, it's different when they introduce you instead as a guy with a low-rated morning talk show."

But at the same time that cancellation appeared to be inevitable, the ratings began to creep up. David *was* finding his audience, and they were turning out to be a faithful bunch. Jack Rollins tried to explain the contradiction. "The problem is that the national ratings did not reflect our improvement. We were doing much better, but we had lost so many markets that the national ratings didn't reflect the improvement. In cities where we didn't have defections, our ratings were climbing dramatically." The trouble was that those improving ratings had to be averaged in with the zeros from cities that had dropped the program. Thus the national ratings were still disastrous.

And even David Letterman conceded that the disadvantages of that morning time slot were probably insuperable. "In truth, I'm not sure that this show is something you want to watch at ten in the morning. But I decided I would try to do the things I like to do. It was always my feeling that if you do a show as interesting as you can make it, and as funny as you can make it, you could put it up anytime and people will watch it." But housewives were perhaps not his natural audience. The NBC brass kept explaining to David how to attract morning viewers, with more "dumbed-down" features. Merrill Markoe responded with irritation: "They're always telling me what women want to watch. They can't tell me. I have all the respect in the world for women." That showed, as Gloria Steinem noted. She told David, "I want to thank you for having the intelligence to know that women at home have brains and like comedy as well." But even though they like it, they may not want to watch it at that hour of the morning. And, unlike the average talk show, David's needed to be listened to. It was hard to leave the room to put away the laundry and then come back again and understand what was happening by that time. The fast pace and the unlikely juxtapositions probably required more concentration than the time period could generally afford. As Barry Sand put it, "Ten a.m. is the Bermuda triangle of time slots."

The unsurprising announcement that NBC was canceling the show came on Septemeber 29, but the last show didn't air until October 24, 1980. David tried to take it philosophically. "This is the hardest I've worked on anything in my life for any length of time. At least I now know in my heart that I did the best I could and tried the hardest. . . . I think you ought to get points for trying." But the experience couldn't help but be demoralizing. "It was depressing when we knew the cancellation was coming," he told the *New York Times* the day before the final show aired. "But now that our ratings have been going up, it seems sort of ludicrous. It's as if you finally unplug the life-support system on a guy, and then he gets up and walks away."

In the days after the show was officially canceled, the atmosphere on the set was especially electric. There was such a demand for tickets to the studio audience that people were sitting all over the stairs, doubled up two to a seat, standing at the back of the room. Many of them had homemade signs proclaiming their devotion to the show, and their unflattering opinion of the network execs who killed it. The guest list seemed more dazzling than ever; for example, one show that took place just a few days after the announcement of cancellation featured Father Guido Sarducci, Isaac Asimov, and a constantly running dry-ice machine. The truth of the matter was that cast, crew, and audience alike were bordering on mild hysteria.

The vitality inherent in the show was apparent to most onlookers. Many people agreed with the conclusion reached by the *Times*'s Tony Schwartz. "Letterman afficionados should be able to argue a case study in faulty scheduling. It is hard to imagine that there is not an audience, probably not housewives and perhaps late-night, for a talk show host whom critics have called one of the cleverest, quickest and least predictable comedians around." It seemed that NBC agreed. Although they were axing this show, it was reported that they had assured David a new slot would be found for him. And soon David had more than a sheaf of good personal notices to make him feel better. When the Emmy Awards for 1980 were announced the following late spring, lo and behold, David Letterman's name led the list. He won an Emmy for best daytime talk show, and Merrill won an Emmy for outstanding achievement in writing. The awards came as an additional vindication of the show.

But there was no doubt that the show's demise was hard to accept. David said that even after they won the Emmys, he remained pessimistic about his future in television. "I was on a plane back to California, and I was thinking, 'Now what do I do? Yeah, we won, but now what?'" He explained, "I just figured my one shot on TV had come and gone and that's it and I would be destined to doing guest shots on *The Love Boat* for the rest of my life." Merrill said he was pretty sure he would never work again. "He's a pessimist," she added, "and this gave him a chance to be *really* pessimistic." Dave once described himself as "having more apprehensions than the average person—or the average medium-sized American community."

Back in California, Dave spent a lot of time running on the beach in Malibu. He played racquetball, saw old friends, spent a lot of time with his two dogs, German shepherds Bob and Stan. Merrill found work writing for Second City. Together they wrote and produced a comedy special for HBO. David learned a few domestic skills: "When I realize that I've mastered the dryer and know how to clean the lint screen, I feel like a *real* man." Actually, he revealed, most of the housework was done by a weekly housekeeper. "We think she's either from El Salvador or Guatemala; we don't really know her country of origin. She seems to be clumsy with the language but hell-bent on taking phone messages; she's courageous in that regard. We constantly get messages that Guba called, and we say, 'Wait a minute—somebody called Guba called? Who the hell is Guba?' And it's always spelled G-j-u-b-h-a—holy cow. And she's really not that good a housekeeper; I guess I just assume that if we let her go, Huns would come and kill her in her sleep, I would be ultimately linked to it and it would be embarrassing."

He enjoyed the life of leisure but had certain reservations about the way California encouraged that feeling. "I never liked Los Angeles as a city. As an experience, it's exciting, but living here is like being on vacation all your life. Since I've been here, the weather really has not changed one degree—after a while you'd kind of like to see a cloud." It wasn't like being in Indiana. "There is no sense of community here. If there was a neighborhood like Broad Ripple, it would be wonderful, but there's nothing."

Occasionally David polished new material in a comedy club, despite his continuing lack of enthusiasm for such performances. He told *Playboy* emphatically, "Nightclubs scare me. They're dark and they stink and they're dangerous and everybody's drunk. The only good thing about nightclubs is that a comfortable living can be made in them."

Luckily, worry about making a living soon diminished. NBC offered David the same kind of contract he'd had before the morning show went on the air, one in which they paid him simply to hold himself available for the time that they were ready to offer him another show. There may be something faintly demoralizing about being paid not to work, but it's sure a whole lot better than *not* being paid not to work. At least it let Dave know that NBC still considered him a viable property, even if they had been unable to make that clear to viewing audiences the first time around.

With the contract bringing in a good salary, and appearances in clubs and more guest-hosting on the Carson show, David began to regain his spirits. He explained, "Merrill and I just got used to the sudden inactivity and frustration, and even though I thought I would probably never get another shot on TV, I eventually started saying to myself, 'So what?' and went on with my life."

But within a year and a half, NBC execs called to say they had the perfect time slot for a new David Letterman show. David cracked, "I think this show will be harder to screw up than the last one, but by God, I'm gonna work around the clock to try."

Chapter

7

Letterman Redux

Tom Snyder's loss was David Letterman's gain.

Tom had been the host of an NBC talk show called *The Tomorrow Show* for eight long years. For the first two-thirds of its life-span the show was sixty minutes long and went out over the airwaves between 1 and 2 a.m. Tom had previously been a local news anchor in New York and Los Angeles and had also hosted NBC's news-oriented magazine show (another in a long line of unsuccessful competitors of *60 Minutes*), imaginatively titled *NBC Magazine*. His nighttime show began as a hard-hitting interview program, broadcast from New York, featuring news makers of all sorts, rather like Ted Koppel's *Nightline* today. Tom was thought to have a genial but incisive persona. His gray hair gave him an aura of authority, but his interview manner was more aggressive truth seeker than elder statesman. The ratings showed that his audience was heavily skewed toward college students. In part, that was obviously because they are the people most likely to be up and functional at that hour. But it was also because they *liked* Tom, thought he cut through the bull and asked the questions someone should put to the pompous celebrities and self-serving politicos that make up the guest list of such a show.

But Tom's show underwent substantial changes in 1980, in response to the changes in Johnny Carson's new contract. *The Tonight Show* had finally been cut back from ninety minutes to sixty, thus leaving a free half hour from twelve-thirty to one at a time when NBC though the viewers expected to see something more along the lines of entertainment than real news. To take up the slack, Tom Snyder's show was given a new name, *Tomorrow: Coast to Coast*, expanded to ninety minutes, and reformatted. The talent coordinators began to book entertainment acts as well as news-makers, and Rona Barrett was brought in as a cohost, broadcasting her segments from Los Angeles. The result of all these changes was more or less predictable: a show that pleased no one. The core of old Tom Snyder loyalists thought the entertainment segments were trivial and regarded "Miss Rona" as high camp; the newly arrived entertainment-oriented audience found Tom Snyder boring. Tom and Rona fought publicly (and viciously) over the way she would be billed, and eventually she refused to continue to appear on the show. The only winners in this contest were stand-up comedians, who began a whole new industry of odd-couple jokes about this unlikely pair. And *SNL* started doing devastating parodies of Tom Snyder that simply made him look silly.

To no one's surprise, the ratings plummeted. On November 10, 1981, NBC announced that they were yanking the show. Snyder's contract, which paid him about six hundred thousand dollars annually, still had nearly a year to run. NBC reportedly offered him the chance to move his show to a new time slot, 1:30 to 2:30 a.m., the desert of the night. A spokesman for Snyder replied stiffly, "Tom feels that one-thirty in the morning is just too late for the

kind of broadcast he's interested in doing. Tom wants to
return to journalism. You have to understand that he was
thrust into this entertainment format last year because
NBC wanted a different kind of show." At the same time,
the spokesman conceded that it was "not probable" that
Tom would take another assignment at NBC. The president of NBC news, William Small, was reported to be no
fan of Tom Snyder, believing that he lacked credibility as
a newsman.

In the same statement, NBC announced its choice of
a replacement for the *Tomorrow* time slot. It would be a
new version of the *David Letterman Show*, and it would be
just sixty minutes long. Not only did Johnny Carson en-
dorse the choice of David Letterman for that time slot (his
contract gave him right of approval over the show that
followed his), but he also made his belief in David Letterman even more explicit by agreeing that his production
company would coproduce David's show. Dave's manager, Jack Rollins, would function as executive producer
on behalf of Carson Productions.

It was the break—and the time slot—that David had
been waiting for. "Everyone seemed to feel that my morning show would have fared much better later at night.
And I knew I didn't want the eleven-thirty job—too much
pressure. So the *Tomorrow*-show time slot was definitely
what I wanted. But it just didn't make sense to me that
NBC would part company with Snyder. I always found
him very entertaining. I'm surprised that to date he has
not resurfaced in a similar format." With this tip of the
hat in the direction of collegial civility, David began to
get to work in earnest planning his new show.

For Dave, and many of the people who had worked
with him on the morning show, the experience was something like returning from exile. During the long months
of waiting, they had all stayed in touch. Said producer

Barry Sand, "The spirit of the group was that we were coming back. It was just a matter of time." David explained how he set the process in motion. "We knew what we wanted to do and whom we wanted to do it with. We brought Barry Sand back as producer—he'd been producing *SCTV* in the meantime—and Merrill as head writer, and Hal Gurnee, a wonderful and extremely creative guy who, incidentally, used to be Jack Paar's director, to direct. We hired a small staff of bright, funny, sensitive people who never want to go to the Polo Lounge for Perrier."

According to Barry Sand, when they began to work on the new show, a picture of Steve Allen stuck in everyone's mind: "A man in a suit and tie surrounded by madness." *Late Night with David Letterman* would retain a veneer of conventionality while still providing accommodation for bizarre behavior of the most entertaining sort. Unlike the morning show, there would be no cast of regulars to do comedy bits with the host; the focus would be entirely on David himself (although, as it eventually turned out, David turned some of the writers and musicians into a sort of ad hoc repertory company and then added Larry "Bud" Melman, the deranged man's Ed McMahon). This time out, there would be some celebrity guests, not only to help in the ratings war, but also to give David someone his own size to pick on. "I know we started out saying we weren't going to use the usual couch sitters," said David. "It took time to realize how tough it is to fill four nights every week."

The new show was scheduled to take to the air February 1, 1982. As that date drew near, the host's anxiety was obvious. Merrill acknowledged sympathetically, "He's a man who wants very badly to do great. There is a lot of pressure on him. He doesn't want to fail." Yet David's personal ambition and desire to do well have never blinded

him to the level of significance of his undertaking as mea-
sured against other forms of endeavor. Barry Sand swears
that once during the morning show, he encountered David
walking off the stage after a none-too-successful broadcast
and heard him mutter, "Boy, thank God I'm not doing
brain surgery." About the new show he said insouciantly,
"Our attitude is, what the hell, it's only TV. We'll try
anything once." Dave's effort to keep his expectations
low-key was evidenced by his comment to his troops
before he went on the air with his debut show in the
light-night slot: "Well, let's just try not to embarrass ourselves unnecessarily."

The date was February 1, 1982. The show opened with
an unidentified middle-aged man furtively warning viewers that they probably ought to tune out because the next
sixty minutes might shock and repel them. Viewers who
failed to heed the warning were then treated to a group
of six somewhat sleazy chorus girls prancing around and
waving tatty, colored feathers. They were introduced as
the Rainbow Grill Peacock Girls; "You know spring is just
around the corner when the Peacock Girls begin to moult."
After this absurdly overblown introduction, David Letterman appeared on the stage in blue jeans and a sport
jacket that seemed to have some problem with its fit. He
announced that one of the NBC top execs had just been
arrested in a washroom at Grand Central Station because
"his pride was showing." Then he offered to take the
audience on a tour of the fabulous set of *Late Night with
David Letterman*. He tried to prepare viewers for the pressure-packed atmosphere of the control room, likening it
to the command post of the air traffic controllers; when
he finally opened the door, it was to reveal the staff drinking and reveling, for some reason wearing Bavarian peasant costumes. In the fabled Green Room, the camera found
a huge variety of flowering plants, shrubs, and trees, as

David intoned, "These are some of the very few vegetables here at NBC not in programming."

David's very first celebrity guest was Bill Murray. One review later characterized Bill as looking "puffy and unkempt" and said he behaved like "an extrovert at a party who's had too much to drink." David later explained the background of Bill's appearance to *Playboy*. "When we asked Bill to be on our first show, he said he'd like to do something different: could he come up to the office and talk with the writers and see what they could come up with together? I said, 'Great.' So he arrived one afternoon when Merrill and I were out shooting a remote and brought six half-gallon bottles of whatever tequila was on sale, and he and the entire staff proceeded to get shit-faced all afternoon. When I got back, the place was a shambles: everyone was dangerously drunk; all the lamps were hidden because Bill had convinced them that the fluorescent lights were draining their vitamin E. Nothing had been written and the only explanation I could get out of anyone was 'Bill was here.' And when we did go on the air, Bill didn't want to do any of the things we had finally gotten around to preparing. Instead, he had a sudden urge to sing 'Let's Get Physical' and do aerobics. So he did. And it was very funny." Bill worked himself up into a panting fit of indignation and threatened, "From this moment on, Letterman, I'm going to devote my every waking moment to making your life a living hell."

Shortly after Bill left and the audience calmed down, the show featured that remote Dave and Merrill had been out filming. It was pretentiously titled "Shame of the City" and it featured David prowling the streets of New York to discover a misspelled sign in the window of a deli: *"Planing a party? Try one of theese."* David promptly went inside and collared the bewildered proprietor, dragged him out onto the street and lectured him about the shamefulness of such errors, and refused to leave until the man had promised to make the necessary spelling corrections. "Truly," Dave concluded somberly, "a shame of the city."

The next guest was Don Herbert, better known as "Mr. Wizard." The Wiz and David ran through a few science experiments together, as Dave adopted his best "Gosh look what we're doing on live TV America" attitude. The show closed with a typical Letterman touch. He brought out a young man who recited from memory lines from the script of *Bowery at Midnight*, an old Bela Lugosi horror film, unknown to all but film cultists. Yes, America, that's entertainment!

Just to make sure people understood that the debut show was no accident, other shows in the first week included such interesting moments as an interview with baseball great Henry Aaron that was followed by a second interview when he was caught leaving the building and asked by a sports journalist what he *really* thought of David Letterman as a talk show host; an appearance by singer Warren Zevon; a stupid pet trick in which a white rabbit named Thumper rode a skateboard across the set; and some wonderful moments of comic repartee with *SCTV* stars John Candy and Joe Flaherty. Dave wanted to make sure that the show lived up to its publicity slogan: "Expect the unexpected."

The show was taped at five-thirty. It's hard to book guests and get an alert studio audience at 1 a.m.; as Dave explained, "In New York at that time of night you'd get people trying to get warm—or looking for a place to reload their weapons." Nevertheless, it had a live feel. David commented, "*Late Night* is a live show on videotape. You've got to keep the tape rolling no matter what; otherwise you lose that element of jeopardy. And once that's gone, you may as well bring in props and sets and dancers and start doing the *Barbara Mandrell Show*." In fact, some of the best moments of the show came when David tried to cope with the unexpected on the air. When one celebrity guest was late, Dave dragged the segment producer, writer Gerard Mulligan, on the air and asked him what he thought the guest would have said had he been there. After some minutes of this bizarre interview, David was notified that the absent guest's manager was backstage, and he asked the guy to come out. When the manager refused, David took the cameras back to the Green Room and talked first to the manager and then to the other guests who were sitting around waiting to go on. David's attitude is, "I love stuff like that. When something collapses, it's fun to see what I can build out of the wreckage."

Most of the early reviews conceded that what David thus built was pretty entertaining. Tony Schwartz in the *New York Times* began with a caveat about the Bill Murray interview. "Unfortunately, the satire was so under-stated—and Mr. Letterman himself remained so deter-minedly in the background—that the show lacked some of the excitement and brashness one might have wished for. Mr. Letterman's presence grows out of his quickness with quips, but he seemed too willing this time to play the straight man." Schwartz concluded more positively. "While Mr. Letterman's first effort was uneven, it seems fair to assume that the show will need time to hit its stride. Mr. Letterman's style is low-key and laid back—there is none of Steve Martin's physical outrageousness, or even Mr. Carson's flinty political edge—and so he is more of an acquired taste than most comedians. Indeed, it's worth remembering that back when Mr. Letterman was doing his morning show, it was several weeks before he relaxed into the loopy informality that makes him so whimsically and unpredictably appealing."

TV Guide's Robert MacKenzie also had a slightly critical tone but still paid homage to David's talent. He said, "I don't remember much that I saw on television in the past month, but several moments I do remember happened on NBC's *Late Night with David Letterman*. I didn't *like* all of them, but I remember them. . . . Letterman is trim, smirky, quick-witted and cocky. Like him or not, he is one of the more interesting talents to come along in a decade. . . . Late night is better territory for Letterman's restless, eccentric style. Nobody is likely to tune him in by accident, and his fans probably include people awake and wired after midnight. New York is the right place too. Some of the funniest moments are taped inserts, in which Letterman roams quixotically around the city, righting dubious wrongs. . . . Letterman has some notable flaws, including a rather big one for a TV host: he is a rotten interviewer. His mocking tone and aimless questions make guests uncomfortable. . . . A man who mocks everyone and everything can be amusing in spurts but wearing in the long haul. Ordinary niceness may not be exciting, but it's too bad Letterman can't be given a shot of it, even if they have to hold him down."

The *New York Post* was brief and to the point. Giving the new show a grade of A-minus, the reviewer concluded, "If this is a hip generation's Carson show, Letterman hasn't done it off the cuff. His taped bits like 'Shame of the City' were cheeky and fine. Letterman works hard without showing the sweat. Get thee behind me, Don Rickles." Speaking of the hip generation, here's what one of its representatives, Andrew Kopkind, had to say about David Letterman in the *Soho News*. "The *zeitgeist* hasn't had its own network television slot for several seasons—not since it flew away with the original Not Ready For Prime Time Players from that old Saturday night stand. . . . Now, all of a sudden and when it was least expected, the *zeitgeist*'s option has been picked up by NBC and installed in the *Late Night with David Letterman* show. . . .

If there was any doubt that the generational urge had at last found a new home, it was surely dispelled on Day 4 of the *Late Night* series when Letterman introduced a white rabbit named Thumper who proceeded to ride a skateboard across the set. The right stuff.'' Kopkind went on to muse, "Letterman is now the official host for the baby boom culture, the audience of videonauts that laughs at sick jokes, makes sense of idiotic images and feels comfortable suspended off the wall. It's an audience that was weaned on *Mad* magazine, warmed up with recreational drugs, and trained to respond to the merest remark of Steve Martin. To these aging freaks, domesticated hippies and nostalgic iconoclasts, Carson or Cavett are not just conventional; they're incomprehensible. . . . It was left for NBC's new chairman, Grant Tinker (the ex-Mr. Mary Tyler Moore) to heave-ho Tom Snyder and Rona Barrett—two exemplars of a dying culture if there ever were any—and give Letterman the post-Carson post-midnight period. The idea was to replace Snyder's audience of geriatric insomniacs with a new group of juvenile nightpeople; that is, to cultivate a group that stays up late by choice rather than pathology. It seems to have worked. Word of mouth during Letterman's first week was *hot*; not since the early *SNL* days has a new program found so much resonance in the 'media-active' demographics.''

James Wolcott of *The Village Voice* was an early guest on the show and a generally favorable reviewer as well. "Like Johnny Carson, David Letterman is a comic with droll timing, flip-top wit, and a sure sense of how far he can push a suggestive joke without offending the sensibilities of the more conservative sleepy-pies out there in the great American heartland. He isn't, however, a bounding, wacky soul—the sort of performer who enjoys swinging from the chandelier. He's more of a sneak wisecracker, flipping off funny quick comments like a pitcher with a deft pick-off move. . . . The show's writers and producers are striving for the uninhibited zaniness of the old Steve Allen show, and in these humdrum television days a spritz of hip humor is certainly welcome. But so far, the comedy on *Late Night* doesn't have a loose spontaneous swing to it, a bubbling up of exuberance. It's *programmed* craziness, and the crackle of stress and tension which dances along the edge of the show's antics tightens up one's responses. Everybody connected with the show is trying so hard to be flip and entertaining that you feel anxious for them, even protective. . . . If it sounds as if I'm being scoldingly severe with *Late Night*, it's because I really do enjoy David Letterman's understated style and sorely want the show to succeed."

One of the most critical of all the reviews appeared in *Variety* (surely another representative of what Andrew Kopkind labeled a dying culture). In evaluating the opening show, *Variety* called the monologue flaccidly written, described the show's humor as feeble, and characterized David's interview with Bill Murray as straining for laughs and failing to get them. The writing was termed bad, and David was depicted as "visibly uncomfortable." Somehow, after all this negativity, the reviewer managed to conclude, "But with his casual, unpredictable sense of humor, Letterman is an amusing man. His low-key, slightly off-kilter way of looking at things seems well suited to a late-night time slot." Even the bad reviews, in other words, predicted that the show would be a success in its time slot.

And the predictions were correct. The Nielsens soon confirmed it. *Late Night with David Letterman* achieved a 2.7 rating and a 14 share, both good showings for the late-night audience when network television has to compete with independent stations' old movies (like *Freeze-Dried Movies*) and reruns of sit-coms. That was, in fact, about twice the number of people who had watched Tom

Snyder. Better yet was the demographic breakdown of that audience. About half of the viewers were in the coveted eighteen-to-thirty-four age group, the people who set the trends and consider most of their income to be disposable. Sponsors began to sit up and take notice. NBC was able to start raising the price of commercial time on the show.

NBC also discovered that the people who watched David Letterman were loyal fans who talked about the show a lot. Within weeks, NBC's director of East Coast programming, John Maas, was telling reporters enthusiastically, "This is the Number One college show in the country. It's a cult already. People talk and say, 'Didja see what they did last night on Letterman?' I mean they *reeeeeally* love him." David balks at the thought that his is a cult show. "Cult brings to mind a curious kind of people living in tents outside of Barstow."

David regarded the threat of tremendous success uneasily. "Privately, I think that I'm not really somebody who has a network television show. Celebrities are other people—Johnny Carson and Sylvester Stallone. I'm just a kid trying to make a living is the way I feel. Here I am, waiting for the fat kid to put unleaded gas in my car, and I'm asking him if I can do it because he's having trouble resetting the pump, and I think, I'm not really that person on television. It always surprises me that what I do in New York between 5:30 and 6:30 p.m. will show up later that night in Albuquerque and Seattle. It's like tossing a rock into a pond and watching the ripples cross the water. I don't like to think about it—it's a little more responsibility than a guy would want."

In his interview with former classmate Debbie Dorman Paul, David was more explicit about his reservations regarding success in his chosen profession. "I don't know that mass popularity and acceptance on American tele-

vision really means that much (aside from untold wealth).
It's more important for me to shoot for something select
than to be on a show like *The Jeffersons*. My aim is to try
to do something different and do it well. The basic premise
of television is 'Let's sell Pintos. Let's get everybody in
this country to buy a damned Pinto. Now how are we
going to do it? Well, we're going to get Suzanne Somers
and eight other girls with big chests and we're going to
sell Pintos.' That's what American television is. I'm not
sure that to succeed in that is such a pat on the back.''

David's own definition of success was geared to the
long rather than the short run. "What I'd like is for this
show to stay on long enough to become just a pattern of
American television. If we're still on the air in five years,
then I'll think of it as a success. The reason Carson has
been on the air for twenty years is not because he does
a *great* show every night. He has his great shows, and he
has his awful shows, like everybody else. But the reason
The Tonight Show succeeds is because people like *him*. They
don't really turn the show on to see whoever Johnny has
as guests. They turn on to the show to see Johnny.'' He
said he wasn't sure that would really happen with *Late
Night*. "I think there may be more going on than the
average person at home who's about to go to sleep wants
to watch, but then again, what do I know?'' David summed
up his own view of what the show really was. "We're
just trying to have a good time. There are places for thought-
provoking material, but not on our show. Maybe *Nightline*. It's really frivolous. It's a silly show. And by design.''

The smell of success didn't abate David's usual apprehensions. *Rolling Stone* reported a conversation between him and producer Barry Sand a few months after
the show was on the air. Barry walked into David's office
and David immediately asked, "What's happening? Is
anything wrong? Has anything gone haywire?'' Barry as-

sured him that to the contrary, everything was going well. David persisted, "Anything exploded in our faces?" In other words, David Letterman is not one of the world's real casual guys, and being on network television, even in a show that is considered successful, can be nerve-wracking. Merrill commented, "The hard part about television is to be evaluated every day. There's no other job where that would happen, where every day you would either have a success or a failure." She added, "Dave's very self-critical. He goes nuts after a show if he sees himself stammer for a second on the tape." Yet one of Dave's strengths is his ability to maintain his perspective. "When you get right down to it," he opines, "we're trying to fill up four hours a week. I mean, it's just American TV. It doesn't have to be perfect. We'll be back the next night." David Letterman's ability to walk the tightrope between his own performance anxieties and his perception that there is something after all supremely unimportant about being on television four times a week for an hour after midnight is what gives his show its special character.

Chapter

8

*He Gets by with
a Little Help
from His Friends*

Television is essentially a collaborative medium. Although *Late Night* is certainly focused around David Letterman's point of view and performing talents, he doesn't create the show all by himself. It requires the teamwork of scores of people to produce the illusion that David is effortlessly being himself in public.

Perhaps most important to the final shape of *Late Night with David Letterman* is Merrill Markoe. For the first several years of the show's existence, she held down the post of head writer (as she had done on the morning talk show too). She explained, "I seemed the logical choice. I had been trained to reflect his comedy." Recently, she gave up the head writing job in favor of a slot as associate producer, specializing in film clips done on location—the remotes—and all the segments that are oriented toward pets. The change in responsibilities gives her more time to work on independent projects of her own (she confesses to wanting to write some things that don't come out of the mouth of David Letterman), and it also reduces some of the pressures that inevitably come with living and working together. "You don't want your boyfriend making all the decisions about your work," she comments reasonably. "I was in daily battle with him."

Whatever battles over work Dave and Merrill have are confined to the small specifics. On the major concepts they see eye to eye. In fact, Merrill may understand even better than does Dave what makes his humor work; it's easier for her to achieve the distance needed for perspective. "His sensibility was, and is, 'You and me know *he's* nuts.' Dave and the audience are united in the knowledge that they're in on the joke. And he's been able to do that ever since I first saw him at the Comedy Store." Merrill saw her mission as creating the situations in which that ability can be utilized at its best. "The only rule is that everything the writers do has to fit Dave's style—all the things he can create off of." She labels that style of comedy "perceived reality."

One of Merrill's key contributions is to find the reality that Dave can perceive the humor in. "I'm the only person who actually reads the phone book. I find stuff in here for the show that you just can't imagine would exist," she told a reporter for *Rolling Stone*. She demonstrated by showing him an ad for a dance studio that promised, "If you can walk, we will make you a popular dancer in three hours." That's the kind of premise that makes her live remotes a continual highlight of *Late Night*. She can imagine dispatching some member of the studio audience or person selected at random off the New York streets to the dance studio to see what would happen to him or her in three hours. Such a premise is funny only if David appears to take it absolutely seriously, or at least to assume that the dance studio takes it absolutely seriously and will really set out to transform the customers who walk through their doors.

One of Merrill's best ideas for a remote came when they were having trouble getting their cable TV hooked up and someone had to stay home to wait for the installer. The upshot was a show with a remote host: Dave sat at home in Connecticut (accompanied by a couple of mini-cams) and tried to get his cable installed while the show went on as usual in Rockefeller Center.

At times, Merrill is a few too many steps ahead of David Letterman in regard to what is or might be funny. For example, one of the early remotes she did she named "The Man Called Jimmy." "I just went everywhere that had the name Jimmy. The whole day, Dave kept saying to me, 'It's never going to work. It's never going to see the light of day.' " But it did, as did innumerable other of her ideas, such as an interview with Mr. Limousine, "The Wonderful World of Plastics" and, a Letterman classic, "Alan Alda: A Man and His Chinese Food." Dave, in a hilarious bit of "investigative journalism" queried the proprietor of a Chinese restaurant in which Alda was purported to eat about the star's likes and dislikes, skill in handling his chopsticks, and so on. Almost nothing was learned, but then that's the way Dave likes it.

Merrill, herself a dog lover who says she misses terribly their German shepherds Bob and Stan when she has to be away from them, remains firmly in charge of "Stupid Pet Tricks," a favorite not only with most viewers but also with the host. Merrill says they didn't realize at first, when they had the "Stupid Pet Tricks" segment on the morning show, that it would be a regular thing. But it was such a hit that the relentless hunt for untapped animal talent continues to this day. David's secret ambition is to get his own dogs on the segment. "Bob sounds exactly the way I do when he eats potato chips," says Bob's owner in defense of his talent. "And if you give

Stan the names of three early television comediennes—
Bea Benadaret, Vivian Vance, and Lucille Ball—the one
he always chooses as his favorite is Lucille Ball. That, of
course, comes not from watching fifties television but from
his association of the word 'ball' with endless hours of
fun. Nevertheless, it's a wonderfully stupid pet trick to
sit Stan down and say, 'Okay, Stan, who did you like
best? Did you like Bea Benadaret?' And of course there
will be no response from Stan. So then you say, 'How
about Vivian Vance?' Again, nothing from Stan. 'Stan,
one more name: Lucille Ball.' And suddenly he's up, running and jumping and making whelping noises. Now,
you tell me: If that's not a network quality stupid pet
trick, what is?" Dave's own nominee for the best stupid
pet trick that's been on the air (as opposed to taking place
in his own home)? "That would have to be the guy who
trained his dog to go to the 7-Eleven store with a ten-
dollar bill in a rubber band around its paw. The dog would
pull a six-pack out of the cooler and put it on the counter.
The cashier would take the money, put the change and
the beer in a bag, and the dog would carry the bag home
in its mouth." Network-quality television indeed.

Now that Merrill confines herself to "Stupid Pet Tricks"
and the remote features, the job of head writer has been
taken over by Steve O'Donnell. Merrill regards the transition as a successful one: "Steve handles Dave so well,
we don't even talk about the show anymore." Steve
O'Donnell is a man in his mid-thirties, one of several
Harvard graduates on the *Late Night* staff. He edited the
Lampoon at Harvard and then arrived in New York in
search of work, which he eventually found on the staff
of the library of the Museum of Broadcasting, a great
opportunity to familiarize himself with the golden past of
television. A fan of David's ephemeral morning show, he
applied for a writing job when he heard that a late-night

version was in the works. Interestingly, Steve somewhat resembles Dave physically, another clean-cut Midwesterner (he grew up in Cleveland) who seems just a bit bemused by the strange land in which he finds himself. Obviously, writing for Dave means being able to look at things from his perspective, so the similarities are understandable. "At the core," explains Steve, "we [writers] all share Dave's sensibility. We aren't Letterman clones, but we are a lot like him. We just aren't the cliché, and neither is he, of what television is all about."

Steve tried to explain to *Newsweek* exactly what David Letterman's humor was all about. "Take the Giant Doorknob," he urged. "Maybe in the 1930s some comic had a prop that was a giant doorknob and his take on it was: 'WAAAH! IT'S GOOFY!!' It's different with Dave. Here's a guy standing there on network television saying calmly, 'This doorknob is really large. It's much bigger than it ought to be. It's *just plain big*.' I don't know. Maybe every generation reinvents the wheel for itself. Or the Giant Doorknob."

Putting David Letterman squarely at the center of the show creates a lot of humorous possibilities, but it also entails some limitations as well. "The writers have basically one narrow personality to deal with," ruminates O'Donnell. "David is ostensibly limited. He's not going to put on funny hats, and he's not going to do one of his lovable characters. He doesn't do a Freddy the Freeloader or something like that. He is himself, and he is king of this particular kingdom. He's this neutral entity that seeks to comment fairly archly on what's whirling around him. He's the soul that oversees it all." Staff writer Randy Cohen explains, "There's no Jewish humor, no black humor, no politics. It's all Dave."

The need to make everything work for Dave means that a lot of bright ideas simply can't be used. On a show

like *Saturday Night Live* or even *The Tonight Show*, an idea
for a funny character can blossom into a full-blown sketch
in which some actor (and Johnny Carson *is* an actor) brings
that character to life. But as Steve O'Donnell pointed out,
Dave doesn't do funny characters. He may *interview* them,
but he won't play them. So some wonderful ideas lead
nowhere. Writer Sandy Frank says, "The only problem
here is that . . . sometimes you'd like to do something
that just doesn't fit. You wish it could. Dave doesn't have
characters. I might want to do something like you'd see
on *Saturday Night Live*. You've got a constant struggle
because you can't do it." O'Donnell claims that around
Late Night, ideas are like North Koreans in trenches waiting to be shot down. Writer Fred Graver says glumly, "I
did not intend to have a job that was this hard."

The writers all joke about who is or is not the victim
of job burnout. For example, in their own book *Late Night
with David Letterman: The Book*, there was a section called
"Let's Meet the Writers," by Jeff Martin. O'Donnell was
described this way: "Though he is more often than not a
burnout victim, Steve's face still lights up at the sight of
a well-tuned joke written on a crisp twenty-dollar bill."
Steve admits that "you do get frayed. There are times
when you wake up, damp forehead in the middle of the
night, just sort of going, *'Dave! What will we do?'* You think,
'I know. Dave becomes betrothed to a Cherokee princess!'
Just total nonsense." He once had to take three months
away from the show (not even *watching* it) to regain his
perspective.

His perspective is definitely on the weird side. When
a *Rolling Stone* interviewer visited his office, he found Steve's
bulletin board covered with cards bearing cryptic phrases
such as "Human Cotton Candy," "Suction Man," and
"Wedding Reception Etiquette." He was working on one
of the ideas, "Cloning the Talk-Show Host." "It's not even

a joke," Steve explained. "It's just a weird thing that we think would look really funny. What we're going to do is to shoot this mold full of plastic foam and mass-produce these hard-foam life-size Daves. You know, just the idea of cloning the talk show host and producing legions of duplicates. I think that's the kind of entertainment America deserves." Steve laments the fact that Dave continues to resist the use of an evil twin on the show. "How can you not like an evil twin?" he demands. How indeed?

Fellow writer Jeff Martin started his biographical sketch of Steve O'Donnell (himself a twin, possibly an evil one) by saying that "he too had picked up a (in this case, meaningless) nickname: 'Head Writer.' " It is Steve's job to orchestrate the efforts of the dozen or so talented people who make up the writing staff. Asked to describe them, Steve answers thoughtfully, "It's the tallest comedy-writing staff that ever existed; I'm sure of that." It's true, many of the writers are over 6 feet tall. Apparently, to see things from Dave's perspective, you have to be as high up as he is. They are also all male (with the exception of Merrill, when she contributes to the writing). Most of them are under thirty, and oddly enough, many of them went to Harvard. "Half the guys went to Harvard and half the guys didn't," elucidates Steve. "Half the guys have agents and half the guys don't. And the only ones who have agents didn't go to Harvard. If you went to Harvard, you don't need an agent. You call your friends." But Harvard grad Jeff Martin pooh-poohs the value of the Harvard association. "I'm not even slightly aware of any Harvard connection. What do you think, I went to Steve O'Donnell and said, 'Any room in your club?' " David Letterman has his own ideas about what the staff writers have in common. "To write this stuff, you have to watch a lot of bad TV."

Among the previous careers abandoned by past and

present writers for David Letterman are accounting, bio-chemical research, the practice of law, and marketing for General Foods. Of course, the question of why a grown man with a degree from Harvard and a good future in some steady line of work would throw it all over to work for David Letterman is something only they or their analysts can answer. Matt Wickline claims, "I'd say we have the best of both worlds. We can write what we want, within limits, and really get along. Hey, we disagree. But nobody ever gets into, 'You jerk—you stole my idea.' We don't scream; we sulk when things don't go right. But nobody *really* cares. Why should we? It's just a TV show." Dave's attitude exactly.

One of the best-known of the writing staff is Chris Elliott, who often appears on the show as "The Panicky Guy," "The Conspiracy Guy," "The Guy Who Lives Under the Seats," and, most recently, "The Regulator Guy." Although his fellow writers accuse Chris of being an actor, he denies it: "I'm not really an actor because I can't audition with a bunch of guys wearing leg warmers." He also claims to be much "meeker" than people think he is, and admits that he is something of a running joke on the show. He thinks his characters go over with the audience because he always looks like someone trying to get on the show. The son of Bob and Ray's Bob Elliott, Chris calls himself lucky to be on TV at all.

To fans of *Late Night*, Chris Elliott is revered as the person who came up with the concept for "The Custom-Made Show," which won an Emmy for the writing. The idea behind that show was that the audience would be able to perform an instant makeover on the show. At the suggestion (and occasional popular vote) of the audience, everything was changed. New theme music was created, a new set was designed, Dave was given a new outfit to wear on the air, the guest list was revised, and so on.

Dave Letterman—
the way his fans
know and love him.

Throughout high school and the first summers at college, Dave worked at the Atlas Super Market…

doing who knows what?

Here Dave looks like a serious student—but the photo was posed for the school magazine.

Dave grew up in this modest house in the Indianapolis suburb of Broad Ripple.

Dave (fourth from right, back row) had an insignificant part in the "Ripples" variety show.

In college, a bearded Dave was a classical music DJ at Ball State's student radio station.

Dave won an Emmy for his 1980 morning talk show. Unfortunately, the show had already been canceled.

On the opening show of *Late Night with David Letterman*, Dave strides confidently through a forest of peacock feathers.

Can you guess from the expression on Dave's face what he thinks about conferences with network executives? At left is Grant Tinker, chairman of NBC; Bob Mulholland, the president, is on the right.

Dave turns tables on Johnny Carson, who occupies the guest chair—only the second time in ten years that Carson has appeared on someone else's show.

Dave's guests span the spectrum; that's Liberace on the left and Bob Dylan on the right.

Covered with sponges, Dave was lowered into a tank of water; he weighed 500 pounds when he was lifted out.

Dave confers with his producer, Barry Sand.

Cybill Shepherd decided to wear only a towel when she appeared on the show in May 1986; she claimed it was because her clothes were delivered to David's studio too early and she didn't know what he might have done with them.

The concept of that show is at the heart of what David Letterman does as a television entertainer, which is to demystify the medium. He keeps reminding viewers that what gets on the air is simply the result of a few guys making decisions somewhere, probably in some sort of unstable emotional condition. As far as he's concerned, the studio audience is just as capable as anyone else of making those decisions . . . so let's give them a shot at it.

The senior citizen of the relatively young writing staff is Gerard Mulligan, a man who has actually passed forty. According to Jeff Martin, "Gerry Mulligan has been working for the show for a long time—too long, we sometimes joke around the office. At forty years old, Gerry is not so much a productive member of the staff as a beloved father figure." Mulligan described himself as "burned out" and adds, "Here they don't fire you when you're finished; they give you some sort of executive position." So perhaps the fact that Gerry has been made a segment producer is an ominous sign. Gerry is a holdover from the old morning show and says that by now he knows exactly what Dave will or won't do on the air. Gerry writes a lot of Dave's opening remarks, and he thinks he's figured out the key to what makes them funny. "The basic philosophy of my comedy is to take the smallest thing and blow it completely out of proportion. A new desk for Dave is monumental."

Among the staff writers who make *Late Night* crackle are Randy Cohen, Kevin Curran, Jim Downey, Sandy Frank, Tom Gammil, Fred Graver, Larry Jacobson, Jeff Martin, George Meyer, Max Pross, Joe Toplyn, and Matt Wickline. If you need a guide to telling them apart, remember that Joe Toplyn is the guy who is proud to be a part of a show on which the host takes a bullhorn and shouts from the window, "You! Want to be on television?"; Sandy Frank is the ex-lawyer who admits, "There wasn't room for humor in a law firm"; Randy Cohen is the only writer on the staff who is not a member of the National Rifle Association (and that's a fact); George Meyer is the one who likes his job because "we don't have to please everybody in the United States, just a few sickos who stay up late." Larry Jacobson spent his first three months on the job living in L.A. and phoning in his jokes from poolside; Fred Graver and Kevin Curran are writing partners who were sold as a pair by their agent but allege that they are allowed to go home separately; and Matt Wickline makes the bold claim that he never runs out of jokes.

Obviously, the writing staff's contribution to *Late Night with David Letterman* is a key one. But another person who deserves a share of the credit for the show's success is Paul Shaffer. By now, Paul has become a personality in his own right. He can regularly be seen hosting specials on MTV, and as *Late Night* viewers know, he was invited by Canadian prime minister Brian Mulroney to attend a state dinner for the opening of the Vancouver Expo honoring the Prince and Princess of Wales. (Paul himself hails from Thunder Bay, Ontario.) Paul dutifully reported back to David on his conversation with Prince Charles.

PAUL: Your Royal Highness, I'm Paul Shaffer from the *Late Night* show.
PRINCE: Oh really? How late?
PAUL: Twelve-thirty.
PRINCE: Count me out.

Paul was formerly the leader of *Saturday Night Live*'s band, and he appeared on some *SNL* sketches. But once he joined *Late Night*, he really came into his own. Standing behind his keyboard in a variety of shirts (always too big for him), his little boy/old man's head looks as if it has been pasted on; James Wolcott in *New York* rather rudely described him as looking "with his light-bulb-shaped head and Mr. Magoo glasses, like the son James Watt is glad he never had." On the show, Paul's persona is that of the almost terminally hip musician whose idea of the big time is an unlimited engagement in Vegas. David told *Playboy*, "Paul was originally hired solely for the music. . . . But while we were talking with him, we were reminded of all the wonderful things he had done on *SNL*, playing Don Kirschner and Marvin Hamlisch. And he is a very funny guy. So we just naturally began utilizing more of his talents."

Paul unleashed can be hilarious. He is especially good when he is obviously straining to be Dave's "sidekick." "Marvelous," he punctuates Dave's every sentence. "You're on a roll," is one of his favorite encouragements. One night he intoned, "David Letterman, the press calls you sick, they say you have a button-down mind. I just want to say, you lead, baby, and we'll follow." Better than Ed McMahon any day.

According to Dave, Paul really does love all that old show biz kitsch. "He records the *Jerry Lewis Labor Day Telethon* and plays back Jerry introducing Chad Everett a hundred times in a row. On vacations, he goes to Las Vegas and listens to lounge comics and lounge piano players and memorizes their clichés." Then he comes back and uses them on the show. For example, after one recent trip, he observed how frequently Vegas entertainers offer toasts—to the audience, to each other, to the evening's experience. So when he came back to the show, he kept raising his paper cup and spouting long involved hopes for "the wind at your back" and a "brighter tomorrow" and closing with *"L'chaim,"* one of the few ethnic expressions ever to be heard on David Letterman's show.

Most critics assume that Paul intends his performance to be a devastating caricature of the lounge lizard, rather along the lines of Bill Murray's famous *SNL* bit or the character of Sonny on *It's A Living*. But David says that Paul is not making fun of those clichés but is actually fascinated by them. He tries to explain Paul further. "When people come up to me on the street, probably the most asked question is, 'Is Paul Shaffer for real?' What he does is an extension of an aspect of his personality. So it would not be inaccurate to say, 'Yeah, that's him.' But he's also a very nice man; a sweet, sensitive human being. See? Maybe it is impossible to describe Paul without lapsing into those stupid show biz clichés. You know him, you love him, you can't live without him."

Late Night fans would have to agree. Because not only does he entertain with his show biz musician act; he is also responsible for the marvelous music on the show, produced by what he likes to call the "world's most dangerous band." The *sound* of David Letterman's show instantly sets it apart from nearly everything else on television. First of all, it bespeaks an easy familiarity with the entire repertoire of rock. The band doesn't rehearse a rock number and then conscientiously play it by the numbers; it *is* a rock band, and a damned good one too. The choice of music before and after commercials is often inspired in its match to the content. The correspondence is rarely a literal one of a title or lyrics that fit the situation (a favorite trick of Johnny Carson's band). It's a fit of feeling. It's the music itself that echoes the feeling of what has gone before. Occasionally Paul goes for some old standard, but mostly he pulls things out of the rock encyclopedia of the last twenty-five years. His assumption is that the audience was raised on this music, that it is the listeners' version of the classics. Merrill Markoe once commented about writing for the show, "I spent years watching talk shows and listening to references to radio stars and old big-band people that I never really knew. It seems finally only right that mentioning a rock and roll star's name wouldn't have to be preceded by a long explanation." Paul's musical references take this attitude one step further, and they are surely part of the reason that an entire generation unconsciously recognizes *Late Night with David Letterman* as "their" show. Paul's band never talks down to its audience, never assumes that the music the band knows and loves is too arcane or obscure for its listeners. And for the most part they're right—and even when they're wrong, it's flattering to be treated like knowledgeable equals instead of musical nerds who have to be placated with large doses of Muzak.

Reviewers have called the band's music "restless" and "jumpy," which really means that it doesn't sound like the normal TV fare. Musically, the band is lean and mean. There's a bass and drums for rhythm, a guitar and Paul's keyboards for melody and harmony. No colorful brass or voluminous saxophones (although David Sanborn has recently become a Thursday night regular on alto saxophone), and no solo histrionics: it's a combo, in the best sense of the word, always working together to produce a complete but not overembroidered sound. If it comes across as restless, that's not because it's perenially playing at a breakneck tempo. A lot of Paul's beats just cruise along, carrying you in and out of the commercials in the most painless fashion. The "restless" epithet is more suited to the choice of material and the great variety of arrangements that make every song sound like a whole new experience on that particular program.

None of the other guys in the band have Paul's featured role, but they manage to make their personalities known, and their very presence adds to the impression that viewers are simply watching Dave Letterman hang out with a few other guys and have a good time on the air. The musicians make a good audience for Dave, and they enjoy punctuating his conversation with the occasional sardonic drumroll or plangent chord. The guitar player will, as guitar players are wont to do, sometimes call attention to himself with some dancing steps as he plays, or simulate an attack of ecstasy brought on by the sound of his own music. Erstwhile guitarist Hiram Bullock was loved by fans because he always played in bare feet; like those distance runners from Ethiopia, he claims to have learned to play that way and to feel uncomfortably hampered by footwear.

As an ensemble, the band is capable of doing just about anything. One night they will back up singer Judy Mowatt and thump out the flat-tire beat of reggae as if they'd all been born with dreadlocks. The next night they've got the country sound behind Ricky Skaggs, then a great r & b number when Sam Phillips is a guest on the show. Whether it's the iconoclastic rock of Iggy Pop or the Vegas appeal of Tony Bennett, the band can do it, and do it well. It's one reason the show has been able to attract such a high caliber of musical guests; the artists know they'll be working with a good band that can give them what they ask for.

One other reason for the quality of the musical guests on *Late Night* is Paul Shaffer. He knows everyone in the business, and he has an accurate ear for the up-and-coming. He's been very good about encouraging new young musicians, and if he turns out to be right about their potential, they may pay him back by appearing on the show even after they've become big stars. Paul even represents some of the newcomers who come on the show— The Weathergirls, for example, a duo of abundant black women, who had the hit song "It's Raining Men." The fact that David Letterman's guest roster has included such musical luminaries as Simon and Garfunkel, Bob Dylan, Lou Reed, and Eric Clapton, is due in large part to the presence of Paul Shaffer.

One other person who makes a noticeable contribution to *Late Night* is its announcer, Bill Wendell. Bill's voice, and the strains of Paul's synthesizer, are the characteristic sounds that tell us the show has taken to the airwaves and that it's time to settle down in front of the set. Bill is a master of the sardonic edge on the voice, which comes in handy for the lines he has to read. His lines are often more pointed than David's, and he's the one who does the political jokes and the savage commentary on stories in the news. Sometimes his comments are about David himself: "Here's a man who, if you ask me, couldn't carry Carson's jockstrap." He threatens, "Just once I'd like to get a few drinks in me and tell David Letterman what I really think of him." Bill often plays the role of the bewildered amateur, saying things like, "I made a joke. . . . How about that?" in stunned surprise. He claims to have trouble with the studio audience, explaining, "I come out, announce the show, and then they try and get at me." Dave claims he "looks like he'd be working at a driving range." It's all part of the deliberately low-key feel of the show, and its antiprofessional stance. No Johnny Olson slick for *Late Night*; they'll stick with someone the studio audience attempts to attack.

Those who watch *Late Night* regularly are aware of another man whose contribution to the show is a critical one, and that's its director, Hal Gurnee. Although he is less often interviewed than the writing staff (might it be because he has more real work to do?), Hal is definitely a pivotal figure. With his calm, professional demeanor, he is the calm at the center of the storm. He seems to be the grown-up, surrounded by a group of mischievous kids.

One thing's for sure: directing David Letterman's show is not an easy task. David improvises constantly. He spends more time over some segments than anyone expected, and he adds features to them that keep the crew hopping. For example, one time he had the late comedian Andy Kaufman on the show, along with his parents. Not only did David let the segment run much longer than it was scheduled, he suddenly got the idea that they all should telephone Andy's grandmother, which somehow, as if inevitably, led to having Andy and his parents sing "Row, Row, Row Your Boat" to her over the air. Imagine a director having to cope with all this bizarreness and provide the facilities to make it work with no warning. And this for a man who delights in calling him "Hal Gertner."

Another significant key to the success of *Late Night* is producer Barry Sand. Unlike the typical producer, Barry is a creative talent in his own right. He has written comedy for Lily Tomlin and invented gags for Allen Funt's *Candid Camera*; according to *Rolling Stone*, he even once wrote for a short-lived game show called *Treasure Isle*. He worked with the folks at *SCTV* and with Merv Griffin, which is certainly ranging from the sublime to the ridiculous. His television experience has provided a kind of professional ballast for David Letterman's show, which glorifies the amateur, and his creative input has helped shape its comedy.

It is Barry Sand, for example, who makes most of the final decisions about the talent booked on the show. The talent coordinators sally forth and find likely celebrities, such as Don King or Dr. Ferdie Pacheco, the fight doctor, or writer Calvin Trillin, and then propose the names to Barry Sand, who tries to calculate just how each of these people will work with David. Can he play off them to provide good entertainment? The guest's own expertise is definitely a secondary consideration. As Barry emphasizes, "The priority is on comedy. If we have a serious guest, it's somebody Dave can be funny off. If it's a funny guest, it's somebody Dave can help to be funnier. The idea of it is that if you've learned anything from the show when you go to sleep, we really made a miserable mistake."

Of course, it's not just celebrity guests that Barry is choosing from. *Late Night* specializes in bizarre guests from all walks of life. There was the golf pro who teaches the art of driving and putting in a tiny studio in midtown Manhattan. The man who never changes his clocks for daylight saving time. A special favorite: the man who flew to an altitude of 15,000 feet in a lawn chair (and was nearly killed by a commercial airliner). For a while, a virtual regular on the show was Alba Ballard, a woman who dresses up her parrots in costumes of show biz stars, such as Dolly Parton or Madonna; she has since become a celebrity guest on *other* talk shows and been in a movie as a result of her exposure on *Late Night*. It's hard to imagine where the show's talent staffers find these people, and harder yet to guess how they get them on the air with David Letterman. To a great extent, that is Barry Sand's contribution. He believes that the important thing is not the individual selection of guests, but the mix. "You have to keep the ball bouncing. We're not an interview show. We're a comedy show. When you lose sight of that, the show starts to bog down. You look at the mix and say, well, it might be too much of the same or not enough . . . crazy. People, you know, they act like they're expecting *Meet the Press*, and it isn't. It's *Meet Dave*."

Barry once summed up what he thought the ethos of the show was. "The show is about the disposable, the absurd, all the things that are thrown out in a Burger King society." He always tries to remember who his audience is; the genre, he says, is "what can we do before the

parents come home?" "Our ratings are alright," he explains, "but the main thing is we have the best demographics of the competition. Most of our viewers are eighteen to thirty-four, and they're writing us thousands of
letters, so they're obviously watching closely. Advertisers
love that." He adds ruefully, "My parents don't get a lot
of this comedy. But," he brightens, "that's alright. They
are not up at that hour."

There is, of course, one more person who helps to
make *Late Night with David Letterman* what it is—for better
or worse. And that man is Larry "Bud" Melman. Fans of
the show tend to argue heatedly about which was the *best*
Melman performance. Was it the time he acted as Official
Greeter for New York City and handed out hot towels to
puzzled bus travelers at the Port Authority Building? Was
it the time on the Christmas show (in July, naturally) that
he was suited up as Santa Claus to read "The Night Before
Christmas" and kept endlessly repeating the first three
lines? How about the third anniversary show, when he
was due to present a "cornucopia of prizes" to the first
baby born during the show's broadcast, henceforth to be
"the wealthiest, most powerful child in the world" (so
sayeth David Letterman) and known as the Late Night
Baby. Then there are the cameo appearances, when he
just comes on to say, "This has been a Melman Production," or delivers a pitch for Melman Bus Lines. Oh, there
are a thousand ways to know and love Larry "Bud."

In real life, Larry "Bud" is actually an actor in his
sixties named Calvert DeForest, a largely unemployed actor in fact. Before *Late Night*, he subsisted principally on
a part-time job as a receptionist in a drug rehabilitation
center in Brooklyn. He refuses to give up the job even
now, because he isn't sure how long his success may last.
In addition to his *Late Night* appearances, he is a favorite
with student filmmakers at NYU (that's how the Letter-

man people found him), and he was briefly featured in a film with Bill Murray and Dan Aykroyd called *Nothing Lasts Forever*.

Calvert DeForest is either a supremely talented actor or else he's just like Larry 'Bud' Melman. Speculation about this question is perennial. David Letterman says, "I guess we've had more comment on him than on any other single aspect of the show. It's always sort of quizzical: is he a guy playing a character or is that really the way he is? He's an average sort of fellow that people are unsure of." In fact, Steve O'Donnell believes it characterizes the spirit of *Late Night with David Letterman* at its best. The whole intention of the show is to walk that thin line between reality and invention so that viewers will never be quite certain how they are expected to respond. It may take a viewer *months* to realize he's been had. Says Steve, "We love to imagine people not quite knowing if what they see is a joke or not. It's that strange pleasure that comes from seeing network television do something that's hard to explain."

David Letterman is the first to point out that "Live TV is definitely not Larry ''Bud'' Melman's strong suit." He adds, "We thought he was a real odd touch and began looking for ways to incorporate him." Dave counts himself a fan. "One thing I admire about Larry," he told Tom Shales of the *Washington Post*, "is that he always gives it a shot, as opposed to just throwing up his hands. Some nights you can see the first domino go and after that it's just chasing a truck downhill." Dave reminisces fondly about that debacle over "The Night Before Christmas." The problem was that the crew members who pulled together the props assumed that Larry would be reading the poem from cue cards and thus all they needed was a book that *looked* like a well-loved classic. In fact, what they gave him was a French catechism. Larry remembers,

"I only knew three lines of the poem. I said those lines and afterward I saw the book and started reading in French, and said, 'Oh my god, this must be Spanish, no it's French, what am I gonna do, how am I gonna get out of this?' I mean, if I didn't have the beard and makeup on, I would have gone through the floor. So the only thing I could think of to get out of it was 'Ho ho ho, Merry Christmas, Santa Claus, Something came down the chimney.' I was petrified." Everyone else was laughing himself sick.

Calvert DeForest glories in his public recognition as Larry "Bud" Melman. He is now frequently asked for his autograph; he says he is offered lunch on the house (he eats at Roy Rogers and Wendy's) when he leaves the NBC studios. But is he aware that people are laughing not so much with him as at him? He says chipperly, "I don't mind. As long as they get enjoyment from it, I don't care. I can go along with it." From this, we deduce that Mr. DeForest is basically a very nice person.

But what about the man who presents him to the public? Is David Letterman a nice person?

Chapter

9

*Giving and Taking
Offense*

At the heart of the David Letterman image lies a deep-seated contradiction. On the one hand, he seems to be basically a nice guy from the Midwest, with a disarming grin and a boyish sense of fun. On the other hand, it is often perceived that he treats some of his guests, both celebrities and ordinary people, rather cruelly. Some of his jokes seem astonishingly insensitive to the feelings of those who are the butt of them. Jay Leno sums up the paradox: "Dave is one of the few performers who can say something real vicious and have it come across as a cute aside."

Is David Letterman a nice guy who sometimes gets carried away and goes too far with a joke? Or is he a sadistic wit who doesn't care whom he hurts as long as he gets a laugh?

It is unfortunately easy to amass evidence for the cruelty theory. Listen to David any night he chooses to interact with "the man on the street." When he takes calls from viewers, he often ridicules their comments and questions, and sometimes further incites them to ridicule one

another. When he talks to passersby on the sidewalk outside the NBC building Dave makes on-the-air snide remarks about flaws in their appearance as they go by. Such
behavior seems particularly unpleasant when he sits safely
in his studio and sends a cameraman out to do his dirty
work for him, as he did in the early spring of 1986 when
he was looking for someone he could send to be outfitted
in a new spring suit. David made the kind of comments
you typically hear from high school kids hanging out in
a public place as he watched pedestrians move across his
little screen. A dear friend of mine once confessed that
as a kid he liked to hang out the window of his Manhattan
apartment and watch people enter the lobby of the building; then he would rush to the intercom and hurl insults
at them, which of course they were never able to trace to
their source. At his worst, David Letterman produces much
the same effect, and it's not only cruel in its effect on
people's feelings but also suggests the same need for power
implicit in my friend's childhood behavior.

If David Letterman is unkind to the ordinary people
he has on his show, he can be downright devastating to
celebrities. *TV Guide*'s Robert MacKenzie commented, "If
guests start to drown on this show, they get little help
from the host. He'll not only sit there and watch them
go down, but he's apt to toss them an iron life jacket."
One of the incidents most viewers remember is the time
he became virtually fixated on Nastassja Kinski's hairdo.
Granted it *was* a strange arrangement that stuck straight
up off her head, but he pushed the point far beyond any
humor implicit in the oddness of her coiffure and tilted
over into knife-twisting rudeness. When she responded
to his initial question in a way that made clear the fact
she saw nothing funny about it, he kept after her. As
David later explained in *Playboy*, "Out she comes and it
looks as if she had her hair wired around a nine iron. So

I figured, anyone who appears like that on television must be doing it for a joke. You've got to trust your instincts, and my instincts said, "This woman has a barn owl on her head; ask her about the barn owl. But the hairdo wasn't a joke, and she got insulted and withdrew." Many viewers remember feeling almost as uncomfortable as Nastassja. And it didn't help matters that his later explanation (in the same *Playboy* piece) relied heavily on disparaging Nastassja further. He appeared to take the position that she was impossible to deal with anyway. "I mean, what can you talk with her about? Her father is strange. We don't want to get into her teenage relationship with Roman Polanski. . . ." It's an ungenerous defense, and one that doesn't hold water, since he is notoriously uninterested in asking his guests any sort of personal questions, preferring to concentrate on their work or some irrelevancy that will make good comedy.

Sometimes, of course, it *does* make good comedy. Barry Sand praises David as a counterpuncher. "He's one of the greatest ad–libbers who ever lived. He comes back with a quip that you couldn't write in a million years." Dave found himself equally fascinated by Don King's hairdo, and he began the interview by leaning over and asking him confidentially, "So tell me, what's the deal with your hair?" Don took the question in his stride, and the interview was both funny and cordial. Dave explained, "That did work well, but more because of Don than because of me. I mean, here's an extremely nice man who's also a real show biz salesman. He's full of crap and he knows it—and that's what I love about him."

Staff member Sandra Furton admitted to *Rolling Stone* that she spent a lot of her time trying to soothe the fears of potential guests about being ridiculed by Dave. "There's a fine line between 'playing with' and 'making fun of' and people don't always see the distinction." It should be noted that it's not just David Letterman personally who is apt to take a shot at visiting dignitaries; the whole writing staff may take the same license. According to Merrill Markoe, former writer Andy Brecher was "sort of in charge of celebrity cruelty." She mentioned a long letter she'd received from one of Andy's victims, Mark Hamill. Mark said he loves the show but still remembered being the object of one of Andy's jokes on a feature called "Video Fun House": "What does Mark Hamill do 400 times a day? (A) Brush his teeth; (B) Comb his hair; (C) Thank God for *Star Wars*." Other shows may treat celebrities as sacred cows; on *Late Night* they're just another hamburger in the making. Barry Sand believes the show's willingness to tread that fine line between entertainment and cruelty is not a liability but part of the reason for its success. "It gives the show its edge," he explains. If some people's feelings might be hurt, or Dave might occasionally appear to be bullying his guests, it's just the chance they have to take, to get the zingy kind of entertainment that fans consider David Letterman at his most amusing.

It's clear that much of the *Late Night* audience likes to see David take on people who appear pompous or self-satisfied. Those eighteen-to-thirty-four-year-old viewers are quick to scent a phony, and Dave probably speaks for them when he explains why he thinks he is justified in taking the offensive in such situations. "If the person seems defenseless, you have no business getting in there and hurting their feelings. But if the person seems to be an incorrigible show business buffoon, then I think they're a fair target." The only catch to this line of reasoning is that few people book themselves on the show under the title "show business buffoon," so they are understandably hurt when they are treated as such.

David told *TV Guide*'s interviewer that he also felt justified in the way he interviews many of the ordinary people he encounters during his remote segments. "I don't want to hurt anyone, don't need to," he prefaces his explanation. "But, hell, if a guy bills himself as the Mattress King, you can legitimately hold him responsible, make him explain himself seriously—which can be funny as hell." Merrill was a bit more thoughtful about the issue. "We're not talking to these people about their worth as human beings or their hopes for their children. We ask only about inane things. The burden of being a jerk is on us because we're stupid enough to ask about doughnuts [the subject of one remote feature]. It's just a different way of looking at American culture."

Steve Allen, who was one of the originators of this type of comedy that pokes fun at the behavior of ordinary citizens, says that appearing to be cruel is one of the dangers that comes with the territory. "I admit when I did those kinds of things, I would never go for somebody who looked like Robert Redford. I went for people who looked like I could make fun of them. Groucho Marx had that problem on *You Bet Your Life*, but his guests begged to be on that show and were very pleased when they made it. Even when you use people who aren't aware they're on camera, they have to sign releases afterward. You can't put seven rules on the blackboard about what is funny and what is cruel." David also tries to make the distinction about who is fair game, and about what topics to cover. "If a guy has been repairing auto bodies for thirty years and has a wall covered with photos of celebrities whose cars he's fixed, he's fair game. You don't make fun of him. You *ask* about it. You give him the opportunity to show he thinks the most important thing in life is celebrities and their automobiles. We don't put words in anyone's mouth."

It all comes back to what Merrill Markoe has identified as the basic premise of David Letterman's comedy: you and me know he's crazy. As long as you can identify with Dave, this comedy is not only successful in making you laugh, it also makes you feel good because it emphasizes your superiority over the ordinary guy. But if you ever start to wonder how the ordinary guy feels, or if you're feeling a bit ordinary yourself that day, that's when you start to wonder if maybe it isn't all just a little cruel. It's nice to feel superior, but to do so carries the implicit requirement that someone else has got to be considered inferior; it's a comparative state.

This issue of feeling superior may well be a key to David Letterman's popularity. His fans are the viewers who can join him in that feeling. He makes them feel they belong to some sort of viewing elite, and his comments about the other programs on television help support that opinion. He has said he doesn't feel he's in show business but in broadcasting, thus distancing himself from the people who might otherwise be considered his peers. "Show business itself stinks," he says without trying to be at all tactful. "It's crap and it's annoying and it can wear you down." And he has also said that there's almost nobody in show business whom he admires (with the tactful exception of Johnny Carson). A lot of his off-the-cuff comedy depends on the assumption that everything else on television is a waste of the viewer's time. For example, he once embarked on a campaign lasting several weeks to persuade some librarian to drop her suggestion that her community should ban TV. David kept reminding her that she would deprive the children of her town of *Punky Brewster* and reruns of *Foul-ups, Bleeps and Blunders*. Another of the fans' favorites on *Late Night* was the parody of an after-school movie for preteens, entitled "They Took My Show Away," in which an avuncular David Letterman explains to little Jimmy that even though his favorite show, *Voyagers*, has been canceled, "it can live on forever in reruns and syndication" and will no doubt, like all previous shows, be recycled soon—the same actors and the same premise but a slightly different title.

This sort of comedy works only if the viewer can join Dave in feeling superior to the type of person who watched *Voyagers* or *Punky Brewster*. Or to the type of person who would display pictures of celebrities in his luncheonette or auto body shop. David Letterman once told a reporter that he liked the way Johnny Carson used to make fun of the "morons" on *Who Do You Trust?* He later apologized for the poor choice of words and explained, "I was thinking specifically of a man whose hobby was to balance a lawn mower on his chin. Carson was clearly making fun of the guy, but nobody's feelings were getting hurt. I admire that ability. It's not in my heart to make fun of people at their expense, and I would never use the word 'moron' on the air." The impact of this *apologia* was somewhat marred by his conclusion. "But a guy who would balance a lawn mower on his chin—that comes close to the definition."

David continually stresses that he doesn't intend to wound the people he interviews. "We never mean to be cruel. It always saddens me to hear that someone might take it that way, but I've had this problem since third grade." He is often genuinely taken aback by the reaction to his remarks. For example, he told Barbara Howar on *Entertainment Tonight* that he did his show for "the goons out there." Only later did it occur to him that he had insulted his loyal fans by calling them goons. "Oh, brother," he told Tom Shales. "This is the kind of thing that's going to come back to haunt me. The spinning newspaper headlines and all that. . . . I don't think it's smart to say the audience is goons. I don't think you can get elected that way." What he really meant to say, he explained, was

"It's us goons doing a show for the goons at home; and it's Us against Them—you know, the prime-time executives who go to bed at ten-thirty." Moreover, David himself knows what an ordeal the whole thing can be from the guest's point of view. Phil Donahue had Dave on as an honored guest in a sort of *This Is Your Life* show, along with high school teacher Gene Poston, an old fraternity brother from Sigma Chi, and some embarrassing videotape of Dave working as a weatherman. "Boy, was it strange," lamented Dave. "Phil used to get such great audiences in Chicago, but what he's getting here [in New York] are flood victims. I knew it would be a long hour, and boy was it ever. It was so bizarre, my heart sank. I just wanted to go home."

All the evidence suggests that on his own show David Letterman does not intend deliberately to hurt people or treat them cruelly. Steve Allen speaks for the defense: "Occasionally, he's sort of operating up on another little level. He's not always communicating on the same level as the guest."

Clearly, the issue of cruelty is one that worries David Letterman. "I don't want to be perceived as an asshole who just says, 'Line 'em up, bring 'em in, and let me make fun of them.' They spend weeks booking people on the show and then they leave in tears and I think 'What was that all about?' We spend two weeks getting somebody, and in eight minutes they're out of here sobbing. I think, 'Yeah, another job well done.' " And he points out that if he really wanted to demolish people, he could do a much more efficient job of it. "Believe me, I can cut a guy to shreds, whap, whap." But he never sets out to do that.

Nevertheless, it sometimes happens. It happens because David sees an opportunity for a funny line, perceives the humor in the reality with which another person confronts him. And remember, he is a professional funny man, someone who earns his living by getting off good lines. It's not surprising that sometimes he lets the chance to be humorous take precedence over the possibility that someone's feelings will be hurt.

David understands this truth about himself. He told *Rolling Stone*, "My big problem has been, and maybe always will be, that if someone says something that I feel I can get a laugh by adding a remark to, I'll do it ninety percent of the time. And I know that gets in the way of an actual interview. And I know that can be annoying, and I try to keep myself from doing it, but something in the back of my mind always says, 'If you don't do something that gets a laugh here, this is going to be dull.' What I forget is that just because something's gotten a big laugh doesn't mean everyone enjoys the humor."

It's possible that, in addition to a sometimes controlled urge to go for the laugh, some of David Letterman's seemingly unkind remarks are prompted by his own uneasiness. Dave is still not totally comfortable as a performer, and now he is performing in front of at least four million viewers. A segment may be set up to make it appear that he has just wandered into the little coffee shop that claims it sells hamburgers to Erik Estrada, but Dave knows the camera is watching, millions of viewers are watching, the patrons in the coffee shop and the counterman are watching too. He has a first-class opportunity to make a fool of himself it he doesn't turn the encounter into something funny enough to succeed on network television. Is it so surprising that he will go for the first wisecrack that occurs to him, regardless of the impact it may have on the bewildered counterman?

And the difficulty is even worse when David confronts celebrity guests who are practiced entertainers making the rounds of the talk shows to plug their latest venture. By and large, these people are old pros at what they do, able to field even the most impertinent questions, ignore every remark that they can't use for their own purposes, and make themselves look even wittier and more charming than the host. Now David has been quick to point out that such competition really doesn't matter to a talk show host. He'll be back the next night, with another chance to shine, while the erstwhile guest is soon forgotten. Moreover, witty and charming guests are good for ratings; they attract and hold viewers, and it is the host who will benefit from that help. Nevertheless, it takes a very strong ego and enormous self-confidence to avoid feeling a bit threatened by an encounter with a totally successful guest. And David is quick to confess that he lacks some self-confidence about his abilities as an interviewer.

One interview that he was particularly anxious about was when he had Johnny Carson as a guest on *Late Night*. "I have no idea what I'm going to ask Johnny," he said beforehand. "But," he tried to cheer himself up, "even if it's really uncomfortable and awkward and a horrible debacle and there's bloodshed, that's great, because people will say, 'Jesus. They were both awkward.' "

Almost from the first moment *Late Night with David Letterman* went on the air, there has been a great deal of criticism about the way David conducted celebrity interviews. James Wolcott said in *New York*, "Letterman camps behind a big wooden desk, where he fusses with pencils and waits for his guests to drop by like students coming in for consultation. That's when the show goes into the doldrums. For Letterman isn't really comfortable with people, conversation, the pressing of the flesh. . . ." The *New York Times'* John J. O'Connor commented that David could be "curiously uneasy" with his guests and cited an early interview with Gordon Liddy. "As the conversation proceeded, the snidely arrogant Mr. Liddy began to take a clearly patronizing attitude toward an increasingly bristling Mr. Letterman. Johnny Carson would have demolished this kind of guest with a single quip. But Mr. Letterman floundered badly. Finally asking Mr. Liddy what the future might hold for him, he was told, 'the same as for you in the grand scheme of things—we shall provide a diet for the worms.' An upset Mr. Letterman was left murmuring something about it being 'an interesting experience meeting you, sir.' " You can see how a few experiences like that would make a talk-show host ready to swing out with any funny remark he could think of without consideration for the guest's feelings.

One of Dave's biggest challenges as an interviewer came when he learned that ex-president Jimmy Carter was down the hall making an appearance on the local news-talk show, *Live at Five*. Barry Sand went over to ask if Carter would agree to talk to Dave, and Carter said yes. "What is David going to do?" Carter inquired. "I don't have a clue," answered Barry. "That's pretty much the appeal of the show, isn't it?" responded Carter amiably.

Meanwhile, Dave didn't seem to have a clue either. He worried and fretted and couldn't find an angle for an interview with an ex-president. A serious interview about the state of world affairs was certainly out, but on the other hand, it didn't exactly seem right to get on network television and joke about the ex-president to his face. It was beginning to seem as if the idea was a dud, leading to nothing more than a cordial handshake and a few meaningless words—the sort of thing you might see on other shows, just to prove that they have the drawing power to get such a luminary on the show, but not what viewers of *Late Night with David Letterman* have come to expect.

Dave's ultimate solution to this knotty problem was brilliant. He went and got crew member Al Frisch, a shy ordinary guy who is an audio technician on the show. With this living prop in hand, Dave's confidence returned. He dragged Al down to the *Live at Five* studios, with Paul Shaffer playing "Hail to the Chief" in the background. Stopping momentarily at the door to be frisked (a step Dave insisted on), the pair dashed to meet Jimmy Carter as he ambled out of a dressing room. Dave made it appear as if the entire point of the meeting was to introduce Al Frisch to Jimmy Carter, an introduction he performed with suitable gusto. Al was overcome with embarrassment, Carter was puzzled but polite, and viewers were laughing out loud. Carter concluded gracefully, "This will make my day with Amy. Being president isn't much, but being on the David Letterman show is something." It was a thoroughly Letterman experience for all concerned.

Some of the problems David Letterman's had as an interviewer might come from an unfounded comparison with his predecessor in the time slot, Tom Snyder. Tom at his best was a hard-hitting interrogator, capable of eliciting newsworthy comment from practiced public figures. *Late Night with David Letterman* is, of course, an entirely different kind of a show. As David pointed out, just because he took over Tom Snyder's time slot doesn't mean he took over his show. Yet some people persisted in making the comparison. And some early errors by the staff of *Late Night* may have compounded the problem. Originally, they did book some guests who were genuine news makers with serious information to impart. David commented, "We've definitely made mistakes with our bookings. For example, we had Gerry Spence, the attorney for Karen Silkwood's family, and we weren't tooled to handle him. I've spent most of my life trying to be funny, not studying political science. I'm just not that guy. So you won't see me steal Ted Koppel's guests again."

One of the guests who turned out to be a serious

mistake from David Letterman's point of view was Andy Rooney. He told *Playboy* that Andy was the only guest who really bothered him. "And he was especially disappointing because here was a man I'd admired for a long long time. Years before *60 Minutes*, Andy had done a series of news specials that I think represented American television at its best, entertaining, intelligent—absolutely state-of-the-art stuff. But when you actually meet the guy, you quickly discover that he doesn't just appear to be a nasty curmudgeon, he *is* a nasty curmudgeon." According to Dave, the first thing Andy said was, "I don't do interviews and from what I understand, you don't do them very well, so this should be quite a combination." Then things went downhill from there.

But even with more suitable guests, David has sometimes been seen to struggle. He says it's because he doesn't like to ladle out smarmy praise of their second-rate movies, books, or television programs, and doesn't like to ask stupid personal questions like "Is there a special guy or gal in your life?" Well, maybe . . . but surely he and his staff are capable of coming up with something more interesting and original. It can't all be the fault of the dud guests. Still speaking in *Playboy*, Dave added that part of his problem was that, "When a guest stalls, I get nervous. Probably because I'm so shy by nature, when a person I'm with is low, I get low. If a guest doesn't want to put out, it's very difficult for me to whip him into shape. It's often said that an essential ability for a talk show host is to get things going at all costs. But I just can't do that." Thus if David Letterman can't get things rolling *with* his guest, he may start to roll *at* him. In a sense, this tendency to use some of his celebrity guests as butts of his jokes is merely an extension of his high school behavior of throwing eggs at the houses of the popular girls who he assumed wouldn't go out with him.

And no doubt part of the problem is David's self-confessed shyness. When he has guests who are also personal acquaintances, the interviews are usually lively and interesting, and Dave displays an attractive ease of manner. But when the guest is a stranger to him, as many of his guests are, he is simply uncomfortable. Critic James Wolcott made an interesting observation based on the way the set is arranged, about the nature of David's relationship with his guests. "The guest chairs are cocked at such an awkward angle to Letterman's desk that the guests are forced to twist their necks like taffy even to establish eye contact with the Letter Man. It's as if Letterman prefers to let his glance dart past his guests to roam freely among his director, his cue cards, the audience, the band." Wolcott lays this tendency down to David's desire to be distracted, and indeed it is not difficult to believe that he has a low threshold of boredom. But it probably also reflects his innate shyness and some lack of self-confidence about his ability to deal with the celebrity guests. The cue cards, director, band—they are his kingdom, where he feels safe and secure. Margot Kidder commented on another aspect of David's relationship to his celebrity guests when she accused him of sitting on a higher chair than hers when she appeared on the show. David was quite obviously genuinely distressed to be accused of such a cheap ploy and moved his chair around near hers to demonstrate that the difference in their perspectives was only due to his own greater height. But that Kidder even felt that way indicates a certain lack of rapport between host and guest. David does manage to cultivate the emotional impact of looking down on some of his celebrity guests, whether or not he sits in a higher chair.

One of David Letterman's most attractive qualities is his own basic honesty. If he is quick to attack the pretensions and self-delusions of others, he is no less willing to see problems in himself. He admits he is not the world's best interviewer and says he has devoted a lot of time to working on improving in that area. He has become more skilled in handling the difficult guest, can find ways of making the interview work other than being sarcastic at the guest's expense. He has learned how to turn the sarcasm on himself, for example, shaking his head and muttering glumly that he just knows this bit is going nowhere, or knocking his fist on the camera lens to see if anyone is in there. When a joke doesn't work, he is willing to let the silence build and then try to use it as the basis for a self-deprecating crack that invites the audience to laugh at him, not the guest.

And the honesty that drives David Letterman to puncture show biz hype also allows him to see his own shortcomings quite clearly. "Look," he told TV Guide, "I'm a smartass and have been for some time. I wasn't born that way; it evolves as a way of compensating. You'd get bad grades as a kid so you'd trip the guys who got good grades. Good-looking girls don't go out with you, so you throw eggs at their houses. Later, you learn to do roughly the same thing with your mouth." In fact, it's a classic defense mechanism. And perhaps even now that David Letterman is the star of a television show with high ratings for its time period and healthy revenues from its advertising sales, he is still at some level insecure enough to need a defense mechanism and it makes us like him and identify with him and understand that even though his insults can occasionally cut too deep, he doesn't ever really intend to hurt anyone.

Chapter

10

Does Anyone Know the Real David Letterman?

Perhaps it's his innate shyness, perhaps it's some sort of defense mechanism; whatever you want to read into it, most people who know him personally agree that David Letterman can be somewhat distant. Jay Leno claims that even though he has known Dave for nearly a decade and considers the man one of his best friends, he has never once been invited over to Dave's house for dinner. Of course, Larry "Bud" Melman makes the same complaint. "No, and he better not show up there either," cracks Dave. Concludes Larry, "It's hard to get to know the 'real' David." Barry Sand is another of the never-invited-to-David's-house brigade. He labels himself one of David's closest friends but admits that David possibly may not know it yet.

These rumors about his emotional distance are the personal counterpart of the questions about David's seeming heartlessness when he interviews ordinary people and celebrities. There's a general perception that in most situations David Letterman's brain works faster—and maybe also better—than his heart. Is it true?

To learn something about a man's innermost feelings, psychologists tell us it is always instructive to take a look at his relationship with his own family. And most especially with his mother. (Thank you, Dr. Freud.) David has remained in close touch with his two sisters, one of whom lives in Florida and the other in a small town just outside Indianapolis. Moreover, it's quite obvious that he is devoted to his mother. Dorothy Letterman is a tall, slender, white-haired woman who is manifestly a very nice lady. Fans had a chance to see her when *Late Night* celebrated "Parents Night" and invited the parents of all those who worked on the show to appear on the air. She was dressed in a conservative navy suit and was obviously somewhat uncomfortable about appearing on television. (Dave once said that in his mother's eyes, his success in television put him just one step above people who work in a carnival.) Her son's attachment to her was evident. He kept asking her to sit by him as he wandered from one location to another, held her hand for moral support, and from time to time asked her rather anxiously what she thought of it all. Still, he was unable to refrain from asking her to pick up the bullhorn and speak to passersby on the sidewalk far below about how Jane Pauley was being held prisoner by NBC. She was visibly distressed by this assignment.

Whatever Dave may have been like as a child, it is certain that being the mother of a grown-up David Letterman has its trials. Until very recently when she remarried, Dave's mother was listed in the Indianapolis phone book under "Letterman," and it was the unfortunate predilection of other Indianapolis residents to give her a call and let her know their opinion of the show—and especially anything Dave happened to say about his native city—after it went off the air in the wee hours of the morning. Even his most farfetched jokes about her had their repercussions. For example, one night he claimed his mother had been Indianapolis's first topless barber. Anyone who knows his mother is in a good position to see how totally ridiculous that statement was, and yet there was a certain amount of tsking and clucking that week at the Church Guild. Of course it wasn't true, but should it have been said in the first place?

Except for the occasional joke about her that he can't resist, Dave is very protective about his mother and feels it isn't fair that she should have to suffer the burden of his celebrity. He usually goes home to Indianapolis to spend Mother's Day with her, and it was Dave who proudly gave her away when she remarried a few years ago. If the pressures of a regular four-times-a-week show prevent him from going home as often as he'd like to, his mother visits him in Connecticut (presumably he offers *her* dinner), or he and Merrill take her and her husband along for a week's vacation on a Caribbean island. As sons go, David Letterman has to be counted a good one.

If duration of friendships means anything, he is also a good friend. Dave is still in touch with childhood friends Fred Stark and Steve Browne. Colleagues from his early days in Indianapolis broadcasting also hear from him occasionally. He likes to slip into town unheralded, round up a few of the guys, and head out to the ball park for an afternoon of relaxation. Old friends are unanimous in their agreement that Dave "hasn't changed." Former colleague Tom Cochrun says, "David Letterman has not changed a great deal, but we see him differently." What they all allude to is David's refusal either to take his celebrity seriously, or to let those around him do so. He told *Playboy*, "The thing about success you really have to avoid—aside from going to prison for fucking up your taxes—is letting the money and the recognition a performer naturally receives make you feel like an especially worthwhile person. I have no evidence that I should feel anything but lucky for what has happened to me, and I certainly have no evidence that I'm a better person than anyone else. But most successful performers seem eventually to come to the conclusion that they *are* better people. It's amazing. And it's very silly."

For David Letterman, refusing to act like a star is really a matter of maintaining his integrity. He explained to *Playboy*, "I can remember being home for the holidays soon after I'd first hosted *The Tonight Show*. An old friend and I were doing Christmas shopping in Indianapolis, and some of the people who went by recognized me. One said, 'Oh, look, there's David Letterman.' And another said, 'Are we supposed to be impressed?' And I remember thinking, you're right. You're not supposed to be impressed. If you happened to see me perform and I happened to make you laugh, great. That's all I'm in it for." Ever since then, Dave has determinedly downplayed his celebrity status. He doesn't, for example, accept NBC's offer of a chauffeured limo to drive him in from his house in New Canaan, Connecticut, every morning, preferring to drive himself along the Merritt Parkway (in a four-wheel-drive vehicle NBC leases for him) like all the other guys commuting into the city to do a day's work.

And Lord knows, Dave certainly doesn't dress the part of the show biz celebrity. His off-the-camera clothes are jeans, sweatshirts, sneakers, T-shirts—not a big investment, especially since many are gifts from fans commemorating their own alma maters rather than his. He emphasizes that the preppy clothes he wears on the show are furnished by NBC. Those navy blazers and tweed jackets are not part of his own wardrobe. (But from the ankles down, he dresses himself; those are his own sneakers.) "NBC owns 'em—and they're welcome to them. Sending out clothes to clean is too complicated for me anyway." He says he is unable to cope with too many clothing options in real life. His dream, he confided to *Success* magazine, is "to be able, in one fell swoop, in one visit to a clothing store, to purchase all the pants that I'll need for the rest of my life. That's what I'm working on now. And I thought I had it. I thought the pants I would buy for life would be Levis—32 waist, 32 length. But now, after buying about ten pairs of those pants, I discovered that the length is off. So now I don't know if it's 33 or 34. I'm right in the middle of this quandary. But as soon as I make the decision on the length, I'll go to a store and buy all the pants I'll need for the rest of my life. Yep, I'm pretty excited." Meanwhile, he admits sheepishly that "I just don't have my personal life sufficiently organized to know which shirts go with which pants and have them all cleaned and pressed at the same time. I have nothing but admiration for people who always seem to know that they pick up their slacks on Tuesday, and on Thursday they pick up their shirts. I don't like doing it. I'm not good at doing it, and having people do it for me is one of the *great* things about show business." You can see how wearing sweats solves a lot of David's real-life problems.

His anti-celebrity attitude also extends to his hair. He claims he never knows when to get a haircut, so it's always either too long or too short. "Hair, like clothing, is yet another aspect of life that after thirty-seven years, I still haven't learned to manage by myself. Pretty pathetic, I'd say." Besides being funny, this statement carries the clear message that you won't catch Dave Letterman acting like a show biz celebrity. "I guess what I'm saying is that I don't want to be a show biz asshole. There are enough of them already. I don't mind being accused of being a bad comedian and I don't even mind being accused of being a bad talk show host. But I never want to be accused of being an arrogant pompous show biz asshole.''

He is known to his friends as a decent sort of a guy. Tom Cochrun remembers how Dave helped him get a job in Indianapolis news radio, a courteous exchange of the favor Tom earlier did Dave in getting him that substitute's job in Muncie. And Ron Pearson remembers how Dave went out of his way to warn him about the problems that would come with a job Ron was considering taking in Indianapolis broadcasting. David's choice of professional associates also says a lot about his fundamental decency. His lawyer is no show biz sleaze but a courteous gentleman from Indianapolis who used to work for the ACLU and in Justice Abe Fortas's law office. His manager is a soft-spoken, almost grandfatherly man. His secretary is unfailingly polite to even the oddest caller. There are no anecdotes circulating about David Letterman throwing his weight around or leading with his ego. Friend Jay Leno says the real David Letterman is pretty much the guy you see on the air: basically a very decent guy from Indiana who loves his dogs, respects his mom, and never lives beyond his means.

Obviously, Dave Letterman treasures his status as a regular guy. The mere idea of hanging out with other ''stars'' makes him wary. For example, after one of Dave's appearances on *The Tonight Show* (he still does guest shots whenever they ask), Johnny Carson suggested that Dave should give him a call and come over to his Malibu house to play tennis. It's a call Dave never made. ''I realized I was terrified of actually spending time with him,'' Dave explained.

Instead of leading a celebrity life-style, David Letterman tries to remain a private person. He gets up in the morning and goes out for a jog in the neighborhood of his Connecticut house. Then he drives in to the city, arriving at NBC around ten-thirty or eleven. He works all day with the staff and crew, planning the evening's show, and then he tapes the show in the late afternoon. Afterward, he meets briefly with Barry Sand and/or Jack Rollins to discuss the show and whatever business may need attending to. Then he drives back to Connecticut for dinner at home, a little television, and usually a ten or eleven o'clock bedtime. Gala events, star-studded premieres, dinners out at an expensive restaurant with a fawning retinue of admirers, personal appearances at fund-raisers and nationally televised tributes: such activities simply do not figure in the Letterman schedule. Dave confesses that his idea of a good time is watching the Jerry Lewis telethon. "One summer, Merrill and I had a house in the Hamptons, and we couldn't get the channel the telethon was on. So I built a big roof antenna myself just to watch that one show. A volatile guy in a volatile circumstance with no sleep in front of a live Las Vegas audience at two in the morning—you just don't get that kind of excitement anywhere else."

Dave also enjoys time with his dogs. Fans of *Late Night* are of course aware of their talents. Who can ever forget Bob's "Dog Poetry"? "My empty dish mocks me. . . . Alone. Adrift in this bleak living hell. . . . SQUIRRELS! DIE! GET OUT OF HERE! . . . Will the folks with the food never come home?" And in the *Late Night* book, Merrill portentously shared some of the important things that she had learned from the "simple yet profound way in which they order their lives." The most important of these lessons, she went on, was that "The day is divided into two important sections. *Mealtime*. And everything else." In truth, both Merrill and Dave like to spend time playing with the dogs, or taking them out for walks.

Now comes the scandalous revelation. A little-known fact about Bob and Stan came to light when pet therapist

Warren Eckstein began to publicize his 1985 book *Understanding Your Pet*. Yes, fans, believe it or not, Bob and Stan both needed help from the therapist (who charges $125 an hour plus expenses for giving it). Their problem, he revealed in total defiance of doctor-patient confidentiality, was that they had trouble adjusting to a New York apartment after years of living in their spacious Malibu house. At least Eckstein had the decency to draw a veil over the details of the treatment. He did, however, add that pets often come to resemble their owners and that Stan Letterman is a very funny dog. In defense of this belief, he explained that Stan once stole a frozen turkey and never returned it. Does the hilarity of this escape you?

Since Dave and Merrill and Bob and Stan don't go out very often, preferring to stay home and use frozen turkeys for nefarious purposes, you might expect that they have put a lot of time, thought, and money into the furnishing and decor of the place where they live. Wrong. Dave quipped in a 1983 interview, "I have a house in California that Merrill and I have been living in for five years, and if it were fixed up just a little bit nicer, when people walked in they would say, 'Oh, I get it. You rented all this stuff!' " Dave's lack of interest in a "star" life-style is one barrier to elaborate interior decorating; another is his lack of willingness to spend what according to his Indiana-based estimates are huge sums of money. "Merrill and I did take a decorator there once," he explained to *Playboy*. "And we told her, 'We don't know what we're doing, but we want the place to be comfortable and unpretentious and not too expensive.' And she looked around and said, 'Sure, this will be great. I'll do all the shopping and bring you samples and pull the whole thing together for $30,000.' " Dave concluded with relish, "So I strangled her and buried her next to the hot tub."

Like everyone else who moves to New York, Dave and Merrill had a tough time finding a place to live. Midtown apartments were too small (and Bob and Stan might have been permanently maladjusted). Houses in the suburbs were either too expensive or too far away. Once they thought they'd found the perfect place on Long Island. "Then about halfway through the house," recalls Dave, "the real estate lady said, 'Oh, by the way, there is a man living in your basement. But he doesn't seem to bother anyone.' It was like the beginning of a bad horror movie, you know, Roger Corman. *He's recently been released from the state hospital, and he seems to be coming along.*"

Dave admits, however, to taking an interest in actual construction and claims he'd like to be a carpenter. When they had some structural work done on their Connecticut house, it reminded him of the tree house he and his friends built back in Indianapolis and the endless pleasure of endless building. "Maybe someday I'll quit show business and throw up a development of low-income tree houses."

For at least a decade, maybe longer, Dave has focused most of his energy on building not his house but his career—an interest which Merrill has been able to share. Domestic life has been a distant second, and devoted though he is to Merrill, he has also been hesitant about embarking on a second marriage. He says they are engaged, which means that when they ever get married, they'll marry each other. But he admits to being shy to jump in again. On the other hand, he thinks it might be nice to have a family. Like most people who grew up in a happy family atmosphere and have remained close to their parents and siblings, Dave views family life positively. Besides, he thinks it would be pleasant to have a "normal" life with kids and an annual vacation and all those other trappings of a stable existence that are so rarely found among celebrities. Yet he admits to a certain lack of confidence in his fitness as a parent. He ruminates, "God knows, I'm only marginally able to take care of myself. What if I suddenly got the kid's head caught in a revolving door?" Not one of the usual fears about parenthood, but you have to admit it gives one pause about assuming those big responsibilities. Its effect on David Letterman is to make him defer any decision about marriage and parenthood until some time in the future. "It's sad that at the age of thirty-seven I can still be that silly about an important subject."

Meanwhile, it's obvious that, married or not, he is quite committed to his present relationship with Merrill. When Cybill Shepherd appeared on the show in the spring of 1986 (for some reason clad only in a large bath towel and a pair of high-top boots), she undertook to tease Dave by saying, "I hear you have a new girlfriend." His distress was almost comical. For the rest of the time she was on the air, he kept muttering about how Cybill was going to "have to explain this to her." After nearly a decade of togetherness, his tie to Merrill seems as strong as ever. She explains their congeniality thusly: "We're both intense neurotic people who worry about everything and expect the worst."

Of course, working together has its good and bad sides. She reflects, "I guess the real hard part is that we talk about the show too much. You know, we go to dinner at night and we talk about the show; we wake up in the morning and we talk about the show. We promised ourselves that we were going to try to have a life this time, and that after the show was over, it would be an off-limits subject, so that you would have a normalized situation. But it hasn't worked out that way. . . ."

One of the most attractive qualities of David Letterman is his open admiraton of Merrill's talents and support of her desire to find her own career satisfaction. Unquestionably, she has been a big part of *his* success, not only urging him on and giving him moral support during the difficult periods, but also generously using her own writing skills and comedic perceptions to help him create a television show with good ratings that bears his name, not hers. Obviously, he was funny before he met Merrill; but equally obviously, he hadn't found exactly the right format for his humor. Her contribution was helping him see how to package his natural talent in a way that appealed to the mass audience of television—and to help him maintain the belief that he could do such a thing. Does it sound too cynical to say that most men in his position would prefer to have her continue concentrating on *his* career rather than hers? It is greatly to his credit that he has supported her decision to stop acting as head writer for *Late Night* and to pursue some independent projects of her own. As Dave has pointed out, it is a common failing of people in show business to equate their professional success with some sort of added personal worth; since they are more famous than their spouses or families, they often also consider themselves more important as human beings. It's nice to see that Dave has avoided that trap.

People who work with him seem to agree that he is equally free of the Big Ego on the job. As the star of *Late Night*, he is the one who takes the ultimate responsibility for the way it works. But he doesn't brandish that fact over his employees' heads, doesn't throw his weight around and insist things be done his way just because he said so. He may argue about a piece of writing or a choice of guest, but he doesn't use his star status as a reason for asking that something be changed. He argues; he doesn't coerce. In interviews, he gives the impression of genuinely liking most of the people he works with, and since so many people have stayed with him for so long it suggests they feel much the same way about him.

There is, in fact, a high degree of loyalty to David Letterman on the part of the people who know him personally. People who have left the staff keep on seeing him regularly, look forward to having dinner with him, and continue to desire his approval. Even people who have been fired from the show (and a few have, for pretty self-evident reasons) still have good things to say about him. Those who are still on the staff speak of him even more highly. For example, production assistant Barbara Gaines, who has been with him since the 1980 morning show, explains how important her connection with Dave has been in her life. "If I'm depressed now, Dave will say, 'What's wrong? What's with you?' More than my therapist, who I've been going to for eighteen years, Dave has changed my whole life. He raised me. I grew up with David Letterman."

Merrill explained her view of Dave's personality in a 1980 interview in the *New York Daily News*. "David is more of a worrier when he's at home than when he's here. He's a lot more worried than he looks and a lot less easygoing than you think. He takes the fact that his sandwich comes late at the restaurant as hard as he takes anything." Other than that, as you listen to people talk about David Letterman, the picture that emerges is of the same kind of nice guy he appears to be on *Late Night*. Former Broad Ripple High classmate Debbie Dorman Paul, who is in a good position to criticize since she knew him way back when, concluded after her interview, "He hasn't forgotten his humble beginnings, he hasn't grown too big for his britches, and he doesn't dodge a single question." He's spontaneously funny; sometimes impatient but never intentionally unkind; firm in drawing the line about what he will and won't do but not really temperamental; a self-confessed sucker for "any story about someone's dog dying"; a loyal friend who tries to keep his celebrity from intruding into his relationships. If he is also perhaps a bit detached, unlikely to speak about his feelings except in a joking way, and occasionally a bit too quick to make a jest at someone else's expense, these are small flaws or foibles, not major character flaws.

Yes, let's admit it once and for all and get it over with: David Letterman *is* a nice guy.

Chapter

11

What Makes
David Letterman
Funny?

There are those who laugh at virtually every utterance from David Letterman's mouth. And then there are those (like his former high school guidance counselor) who don't think he's the least bit funny. Which are the folks who should be removed from society?

Analyzing a joke, like all other forms of dissection, kills the subject under investigation. When you try to think about *why* something is funny, you are only a short step away from concluding that it isn't really very funny after all. Nevertheless, it is possible, without doing too much damage to the spontaneity of David Letterman's comedy, to pick out some of the reasons it works. And perhaps as well to see why it doesn't work at all for some people.

One important element of *Late Night* comedy is Dave's love of misinformation: fiction masquerading as fact. As you recall, this characterized his humor even way back in Indiana broadcasting, when he made up the weather reports and consistently mispronounced the name of the state's governor. He is still very fond of that sort of joke.

For example, for weeks he told audiences about NBC's forthcoming magazine show, *American Almanac*, and claimed that it starred (along with Connie Chung) ex-president Gerald Ford, rather than the actual host, Roger Mudd. In fact, NBC is one of his favorite sources of misinformation. He announces personnel changes and executive shake-ups that never take place, gives biographical facts about its employees that are totally fictitious, and explains to the studio audience various network practices and policies that he has invented. As always, Jane Pauley is especially likely to be the subject of his startling fictions: she has resigned, agreed to star in a new program, been held hostage by Willard Scott.

This delight in the inaccurate extends even to the minor detail of names. He will go for weeks calling someone on the crew or staff by an erroneous version of their name. For example, when drummer Anton Fig joined the show, he was first called merely "the new guy" for weeks and then Anton Zipp. Dave loves to call director Hal Gurnee by such misnomers as "Gurley" or "Gertner." The joke is somewhat rarefied, since only other members of the staff and dedicated fans know what Hal's real name is; casual listeners just assume he's named whatever David has called him. It's exactly the same type of joke as calling Otis Bowen, Governor "Bowman," and springs from the same attitude.

Such misinformation is really in the nature of a practical joke. When aimed at a particular person, such as Jane Pauley, it is a form of teasing for the subject of the joke. But the biggest tease, of course, is for the audience, to see if they are going to swallow any of the fabrications. The pleasure in this kind of joke comes from the jokester's own internal chortles at the thought of all those people walking around believing something ridiculous that has been put over on them. In its simplest form, this joke is an "April fool," a statement that suckers the listener into some response and then quickly reveals that he's been had. With increasing sophistication, it's no longer really necessary for listeners actually to fall for it. It's funny just to think that after all they might.

Another interesting aspect of this sort of joke is that it makes an implicit comment about the power of the media. People tend to believe what they hear broadcast over radio and television, or see printed in the newspaper, and they believe it simply *because* of the source. Even when the media tells them something they know to be improbable—that Gerald Ford would be the host of a television news magazine—or downright impossible—that hailstones the size of canned hams could exist—they still tend to give it credence. David Letterman reminds us of the amazing power of the media, and how we will believe something from even the dopiest weatherman that we would scoff at if heard from a friend or neighbor. And he also likes to puncture our illusions about how all the people who work in the media are sober elder statesmen who look like Walter Cronkite and weigh their responsibilities heavily before every public pronouncement. Remember, he warns, most of them are just jerks like you and me. They're just doing a job, the same as everyone else in the audience, with about the same likelihood of being right all the time.

That leads us to another distinguishing feature of David's humor. He does his best to demystify the communications media, deriving humor thereby as well as making a point that is dear to his heart. Or as one critic put it aptly, David Letterman takes the magic *out* of television.

He does it in a million little ways. Did you ever notice how every time he comes out on the stage at the beginning of the program he looks down at his feet to make sure he has hit the mark that shows where he's supposed to stand? Other television stars make a particular effort to give the impression that they have just casually sauntered over to the one spot on the floor where all the cameras will get the best shot of them. Dave makes it plain to his audience that it is not mere accident but careful behind-the-scenes planning that gets him to that particular location. Someone checked it out in rehearsal, someone else made a mark on the floor, and he is careful to stand on it.

Dave also likes to have the camera swivel around to show the crew member who is holding Dave's cue cards when he tells his opening jokes. ("Kevin" is what Dave calls him, though whether or not that's his real name is a subject of conjecture to those who know Dave's delight in getting names wrong.) That reminds everyone watching, not just the studio audience, that Dave's funny remarks are not really off the cuff, the way they are made to appear, but have been written for the occasion, very likely by someone other than Dave. Of course, there's a certain protective element in this attitude: if the jokes bomb, Dave has already distanced himself from them. But it's much more significant that he is willing to relinquish the credit for being spontaneously funny in order to demonstrate the way a television program really works.

In similar fashion, he likes to ask the director to get shots of the various crew members at work. He displays the workings of their mechanical props, shows us how the sound effects are created, lets us see the crew members who are running around the set and the back hallways, gives us a glimpse of the celebrity waiting nervously in the wings to be announced and make that grand entrance. And on occasion, he even likes to show us the functional areas of NBC that are beyond the studio: the elevator banks, the Green Room, the corridor that leads over to the *Live at Five* studio where the local NBC affiliate is simultaneously broadcasting a news-talk show. The significance of these stolen glimpses and tourlike excursions is to demonstrate how much more there is to any television show than what ultimately appears within the frame of the small screen in the viewer's living room. The television viewing experience is a consummate illusion, in which a two-dimensional artifact is present as a three-dimensional reality. *Late Night* continually confronts the viewer with hard evidence of the reality that goes on around the carefully contrived presentation.

Of course, there's more to all this than just making philosophical points. David Letterman is not giving a scholarly lecture on the nature of human perception of reality, he is trying to be entertaining. He makes each of these bits of business funny. We laugh with him over the struggles involved in getting things to work right, and we appreciate his putdown of the pretensions that customarily accompany such enterprises.

For that is another of the elements of his comic vision. David Letterman is a person who has grown up with television and who, like most of us, has spent countless hours watching the well-publicized programs on network television. It is precisely because he has watched so much television, and absorbed so much of its self-glorifying publicity, that he is so good at deflating the hype. He delights in using all those old-time phrases that attempted to connote great excitement. "Boy, have we got a keen show for you folks this evening," he might begin. "Yes, it's a power-packed, histrionic extravaganza! So strap yourselves in. Phone the neighbors. Wake the dog and give it a beer. This is going to be more fun than humans should be allowed to have!" The verbal quotation marks that display his mental reservations about using this high-flown language to describe something as mundane as another television program are always implicit, but sometimes he makes his point explicitly as well. "What a night! Can you feel the electricity in the air? Can you feel the excitement?" Pause. "Well then, you're in the wrong place."

At other times, the sarcastic note is dominant. When some segment is not going over especially well, he likes to remark, "We're doing comedy here tonight, aren't we?" When some bit of business fails completely, he likes to remind his audience, "Yes, it *is* network television." He refers to his viewers as "the vast North American home-viewing audience," and he gives inflated titles to little ten-second gags: the Leap for Life, the Ramp O' Death, the Jello from Hell. Even the coffee cup that is a familiar talk show host's prop becomes the "Cup O' Coffee." All the old show business clichés are suddenly turned into zingers that comment sardonically on the slightest hope that something of merit or value will emerge from such an unlikely location as a daily television show.

Interestingly, it is this sardonic attitude that enables *Late Night* to fulfill all its obligations to NBC without ever seeming to act the part of the shill. Every network tries to use its successful programs to promote some of its other programs (successful or otherwise). For example, NBC wanted *Late Night* to make some mention of the fact that the Phil Donahue show was moving to New York and would soon be taped in front of a live New York audience, just like *Late Night*. This sort of prostitution is par for the course, and certainly every talk show host has been asked to participate in such activities. In David Letterman's hands, such a routine promotional activity turns into something entirely different. He begins to keep a calendar that counts down the days until Phil Donahue arrives in New York, and every day on the air he marks off another day—on a giant blowup of Phil's face. Later, when asked to plug NBC's magazine show *American Almanac*, he institutes a similar countdown, this time using sophisticated com-

puter graphics that flash the number of days remaining
until the show goes on the air and causes the pictures of
the hosts to jump about alarmingly, whirling in and out
of the mist.

By putting these ironic twists on the everyday commercial business of promoting the network's shows, David
Letterman manages the seemingly impossible feat of doing
exactly what NBC expects of him while still retaining the
appearance of great independence and the image of being
immune to media hype. And, of course, he also succeeds
in being funny. Because the pretentiousness of these efforts is so out of scale to their lowly purposes, one can't
help laughing.

The question of scale on television is one that frequently occupies David's attention. That shouldn't surprise us in a person who loves the Giant Doorknob, or
wants to call up the various people who claim to be the
owners of the world's largest vase. But it's not just the
unexpected size of everyday objects that delights Dave;
it's the departure from measurement standards of all types.
One way to interpret the comedic ethos of *Late Night* is
to compare it with the measuring stick for late night television, *The Tonight Show*. Obviously, Dave's choice of side-
kicks is one of the chief differences in professional scale.
Instead of the relentlessly genial Ed McMahon, *Late Night*
has the professionally inept Larry "Bud" Melman. Instead
of Doc Severinsen, who comes on the show talking about
his recent engagements in Vegas and the size of the audience that came to see him perform, *Late Night* has Paul
Shaffer, who delights in being part of that audience and
talks like a star-struck kid about the appearances of old
Vegas pros like Doc.

This scaling down can be seen in many other areas.
Where Johnny has as a frequent guest the glamorous and
sophisticated Joan Embry from one of the world's best

zoos, in San Diego, bringing along rare animals for the audience to admire, Dave has Jack Hanna of the Columbus, Ohio, zoo, a thoroughgoing Midwesterner who says cheerfully that his animals are all still "eatin' and breedin' " and brings along such rarities as a baby bear and a couple of kangaroos. Johnny has a list of "regular" guests who appear every time they have something new to plug, perhaps even occasionally when they don't. His list includes such celebrities as Burt Reynolds, Don Rickles and Tom Selleck: big names in the entertainment biz. Dave does the same thing, but his regulars are such people as Charles Grodin and Bruce Dern—good actors and entertaining conversationalists, mind you, but not top box-office attractions.

And of course, a great number of Dave's guests are decidedly nonfamous, just ordinary people who suddenly find themselves blinking in the limelight. On *The Tonight Show*, to be asked to come sit down on the sofa next to Johnny is an accolade reserved for people who are either very famous or about to be. On *Late Night*, that position could be occupied by almost anybody. There was the guy who was stopped on the street on an early spring afternoon, for example, and then dispatched to buy himself a new spring suit. At the end of the program, he appeared resplendent in his new attire, sat in the chair and chatted with Dave briefly, and then suddenly burst into a chorus of "Tonight," which he said he'd always wanted to do on television.

The way *Late Night* is scaled down from its counterpart *The Tonight Show* provides the foundation for a lot of self-deprecating humor. Dave likes to refer to his show as "the kid brother or ugly cousin" of Johnny's show, and gleefully labels *Late Night* "fringe broadcasting." When some prepared segment isn't working, Dave will explain, "We'll eliminate the ones that don't work, and at the end

of the year, we'll have a compilation of mediocre stuff."
In interviews, he makes comments like, "All I know is
we're not as slick as prime time," or "We are a no-frills,
nuts and bolts show. We don't have big sets, a big cast
and all those colored lights, so people don't expect to see
something special." He likes to imply that this smallness
is due to a tiny budget, or very tight rehearsal time. He
likes to joke, "*The Today Show* is on a cruise now, and
we're working with hairpins." But in fact, his show's
"smallness" represents a deliberate choice of the amateur
over the professional. He thinks it's funny to have cheesy
props, noncelebrities, segments taped on the street with
bewildered real people rather than celebrities all dressed
up in eye-catching clothes spinning their smooth patter.
He mocks the big media event by holding such special
events as "Bob Rooney Day," in honor of one of his crew
members, and having Bob Hope videotape a tribute to
this unknown ordinary guy. It's funny, and at the same
time it needles the pompousness of other shows that take
videotaped tributes by Bob Hope seriously.

To a great extent, David Letterman's humor is con-
textual, as the above example indicates. A cameo appearance by Bob Hope, either live or on tape, is virtually
a show business cliché; there's nothing funny about it
(except what Bob Hope's own jokewriters can come up
with). But when you put it in the context of a tribute to
an audio technician whose name and face are completely
unknown to the American public, that's funny. The whole
idea of the tribute from the celebrity becomes funny when
the context is thus shifted.

Context is also what makes "Stupid Pet Tricks" work.
We've all seen these dopey pet owners who insist on
making you watch their cat or dog do something they
find just extraordinary, such as yelp along with them
when they sing. It's the sort of experience you pray won't

happen to you when you visit new neighbors or distant in-laws. In somebody's living room, a stupid pet trick can kill the fun in an entire evening. But when you see it on network television, it's suddenly converted into entertainment. And *Late Night* makes it twice as funny by applying to it the slick techniques borrowed from other entertainment events: drum rolls to mark the big moments, instant replays so each little movement can be analyzed, audience response measurement to determine the "best" stupid pet trick. ("As always," Dave warns, "no wagering please.") By shifting the context, Dave can take the usually painful experience of a human being making a fool of himself in the immediate vicinity of an animal and turn it into something that is genuinely amusing.

You may notice, in fact, that Dave and his writers are very fond of announcing proudly that "you are seeing this on network television." They create humor out of the gap between expectation and reality. The expectation is that network television means the highest level of professional talent, that the people you see on the little screen are the "best and the brightest" in the entertainment world. That's what the networks would have you believe, and what the machinery of public relations and publicity for all the shows and all the stars on them is geared to portraying. David Letterman then goes on television with a pizza delivery contest, races between members of the studio audience in the NBC elevators, and songs performed by William Shatner and Telly Savalas. And all the while he is grinning and insisting that this is network television at its finest. The best part of the joke is that, in its way, it *is*.

In regard to network television, Dave achieves a comic effect by pretending to take seriously the media hype that it generates about itself. He uses old, tired PR clichés, like "This will be the best television season ever," and puts the phrase in the mouth of a kid to whom he has just explained that nothing original ever actually comes on television. He reads NBC promo copy, glowing adjectives and all, as if it really meant something (and then waits for the laughs from the audience, who realize that it doesn't mean a thing).

This is another key to his humor. He wrings comedy out of the real world by playing straight man to other people's overinflated pronouncements. That's what makes many of his remote segments so funny. He looks for the signs outside businesses in their windows, that most people take for granted: the claim to be an expert in a particular line of business, for example, or the pictures that prove that celebrities are customers of the business. Then, by appearing to take the statement seriously, he reveals not just the comedy of an ordinary guy trying to look more important than he really is but also the implicit humor that such claims should be made at all—and then largely ignored by the rest of the world. Most of us unthinkingly go in to leave our dirty suits at a place that labels itself the "world's best cleaner." David Letterman takes the cleaner up on that claim, and interviews him as if he is indeed interviewing the world's best cleaner and it's an important media event (because it's on network television, you see).

This technique is sometimes called the "man from Mars" approach. It is sometimes used to convey real innocence: it's the way the country rube acts when confronted by the wonders of the big city, for example. It helps that Dave's personality is so resolutely "ordinary," not like you expect a celebrity to be. That he is easily embarrassed thus works for him rather than against him. He says, "I have a real low threshold of embarrassment. It may be hard to tell that from watching the show [he is alluding to an occasion on which he was covered with chips and lowered into a vat of dip]. Or it may be that I'm in the wrong line of work." This lack of ease before the camera, especially in some sort of contrived situation, comes across as the equivalent of innocence.

For the most part, Dave approaches the "man from Mars" technique in a more sophisticated vein. He makes it obvious he is merely playing along with the man who claims to be the world's best dry cleaner, rather than being taken in by him. He expects his viewers to laugh at the dry cleaner for the answers he gives to Dave's questions, not at Dave himself for asking the questions in the first place. It's the old "you and me know he's nuts" ploy. But it's effective because Dave does still have a look of midwestern innocence, perhaps even naïveté. Thus many of his remote segments are really part of a long tradition of stories about the adventures of the country boy when he goes to the big city, a tradition that reaches back at least as far as Fielding's Tom Jones, the good-hearted country innocent who is simultaneously enlightened and corrupted by his experiences in London.

To preserve this aspect of Dave's humor, it is important that he should not be perceived as being a New Yorker, even though his show originates in New York, has an audience that mostly comes from New York, and contains a heavy dose of New York sophistication in its viewpoint. Dave therefore never tires of reminding the viewers that he is from Indiana; and when he talks about New York, it's always with the detached tone of an observer. The nightly intros by announcer Bill Wendell for Dave's appearance are little masterworks that get the best of the show's close identification with New York and still transcend the negative aspect of its image. At the time that the 1986 scandals about corruption in the New York City government began to break, for example, Bill proclaimed that the show was from New York, "one of the finest examples of corruption you'll ever see, and we couldn't be more proud." A few days later, he reminded viewers that there was still time to mail in their bribes to city officials. The usual tone of David's own distance from New York is indicated by another of Bill's introductions: "And now, from New York, the home of a lot of big fat loud guys who spend their lunch hour shouting insults at women . . . here's David Letterman." This immediately puts the audience on notice that David is *in* New York but not *of* it. So he succeeds in keeping his midwestern purity intact, and that permits him to continue to play it off against the strange behavior he perceives in the city.

Dave's ability to confront the counterman at a dough-nut shop and ask him seriously how many doughnuts a day he thinks people ought to eat ("Three dozen" was the surprising answer) depends not just on his image as an unspoiled Midwesterner, but also on his natural boy-ishness. Although pictures show that David's appearance has actually changed over the years, he doesn't have a particularly "grown-up" face. Like Johnny Carson, he looks—and acts—younger than his actual age.

Some people find this youthfulness appealing, prob-ably especially Dave's own inclined-toward-youth audi-ence. Some grown-ups find it annoying. James Wolcott made a good case for this point of view: "I don't mind the silliness of *Late Night*, but I find myself thirsting for something more than silliness. The most happily relaxed I've seen Letterman was with the humorist Calvin Trillin, because Trillin, that droll potato, knows how to crack small whimsies and make those around him feel as if they're part of an intelligent conspiracy. For once, Let-terman actually listened, flattered to be on Trillin's odd, sane wavelength. If David Letterman is going to make the long haul, he's going to have to spend more time listening to grown-ups like Calvin Trillin and less time staring at the shine on Paul Shaffer's head."

There is, in fact, something very collegiate about David Letterman's humor. That probably reflects his own attitudes truthfully. No doubt it is also magnified because so many of his writers are themselves young, and also veterans of college humor publications such as the Harvard *Lampoon*. The sophomoric quality of their collective humor is especially noticeable in certain regular features, such as New Gift Ideas or Dave's Toy Shop. The "hangman" swizzle stick, the whiffle ax, the praying hands raceway, the orphan alarm (it goes off if one is abandoned on your doorstep) and the line of greeting cards ("When I think of all the years we've spent together . . . I long for the release that death will bring") are all comedic ideas that appeal to the readers of *Mad* and *National Lampoon*. The ongoing morality tale of Fred and Frank also contains a marked element of juvenility.

Much of this humor comes across as boys surreptitiously giggling over the way their elders behave—kids in schools laughing behind the teacher's back, or cast and crew of *Late Night* laughing behind the backs of NBC network executives. This is particularly noticeable when the subject has some sexual connection.

Many observers have commented on the fact that David Letterman does not rely on blue humor or crude language for his comedy. In fact, he often makes fun of that type of comedian. One night his opening remarks started out with the first few lines of a joke that was obviously going to be about the size of Dolly Parton's breasts. But in the middle of the joke, David stepped forward, peered at the cue cards, and said, "Oh, I see. That joke was left over from last Christmas's Bob Hope special."

Nevertheless, *Late Night* still conveys a certain leering

attitude toward women. When Dave interviewed the 1986 Playmate of the Year, he made a big point of thumbing through the magazine on the air and appearing to be shocked by the revealing poses. That attitude was reinforced later in the show when he read a piece of viewer mail asking what happens to the old *Playboys* and *Penthouses* after they have been used in this fashion; the answer showed an innocent Boy Scout coming round to take all the lewd magazines away in his little red wagon.

Granted, you don't invite a Playmate on the show to talk about brain surgery. But where Johnny Carson might handle such an interview in a droll man-of-the-world fashion, David Letterman seems overcome by the naughtiness of it; it's the attitude of a boy rather than a man. In fact, it seems difficult for him to treat sex matter-of-factly. This was made painfully evident on the several occasions when he had sex expert Dr. Ruth Westheimer on the show. Dr. Ruth's specialty is plain talk about sexual problems; she demystifies the subject and makes it about as emotion-laden as hints about your auto repairs. She and David Letterman made an odd couple indeed. As she began to instruct women bluntly in the usefulness of zucchini, David's embarrassment mounted visibly. Finally he left the set. Obviously, he was dramatizing his discomfort to make it funny, but just as obviously, he really *was* uncomfortable about it. He prefers to be back in the land of innuendo where he can giggle with the other guys at the thought of "doing it." David Letterman can blush during a discussion about whether someone's dog might be going to have puppies.

Another juvenile aspect of his attitude toward women is his emphasis on the importance of their good looks. When he has an attractive female guest, he usually makes some reference to the fact. For example, he introduced the talented Bernadette Peters—at that point just nominated for a Tony in recognition of her performance in *Song and Dance* on Broadway—as having "the smoothest skin of anyone we've ever had on the program." And a staple of Dave's humor is the joke about the unattractive woman. For example, one night Bill Wendell introduced him as "the man who hopes that scientists will one day develop equipment sensitive enough to determine the weight of Oprah Winfrey." When he had the Weathergirls on, he made much of their former billing of themselves as Two Tons of Fun, asked demeaning questions about such topics as how they found costumes in their size, and made other weight-related jokes. It is often all too easy to hear in David Letterman the high school boy who feared that the "good-looking" girls wouldn't go out with him.

It's not just the subject of sex that brings out this boyish attitude from Dave and his writers (who are now all male and mostly rather young). It's the entire relationship between the sexes. Women are seen as the responsible members of any couple, dispensing instruction, reward, and punishment to their male partners: in other words, women play the grown-ups to men's children. Look for example at the "farewell" speeches from the King and Queen Termite (specimens in jars lent to *Late Night* for a week by the American Museum of Natural History). The queen began a majestic speech full of high-flown sentiment, which was soon interrupted by jerky remarks by the king. Eventually, she started to scold and lecture and threaten him, and the total effect was rather like reading one of the old "Jiggs and Maggie" comic strips. It was funny, but it also conveyed a peculiarly dated perspective on the relationship between the sexes.

It seems probable that David Letterman is uncomfortable in the grown-up world of serious relationships, intimate feelings, real problems that give real people really hurt feelings. He is happier in his teenage boy's universe where the important topics are sports, jokes, and girls. It requires no great power of observation to see that sports, and especially his beloved baseball, are one of his greatest interests and favorite subjects for jokes. His persistent teasing of such major leaguers as Terry Forster, the Braves (and now the Angels) pitcher with the biggest belly in professional sports, and Buddy Biancalana, shortstop on the Royals championship team whose batting average never rose above .189, has turned them into media stars. They've both been guests on the show, and in spring training their autographs are eagerly sought by Letterman fans. A never failing source of comedy on the show is the interplay between Dave, the knowledgeable sports fan, and Paul Shaffer, who must surely be the only Canadian boy who managed to grow up knowing absolutely nothing about hockey. Dave throws off some casual, offhand remark about a game the day before, just the sort of thing that a lot of guys probably said that day at the office or over a few beers at the end of the day. Paul looks totally blank and then tries to play along in a way that emphasizes both his good nature and his total lack of understanding of the subject. It's the old high school pastime of laughing at the nerd, making fun of the boy who doesn't share the average male interests: baseball, football, and speculation about which girls will go all the way.

One other aspect of the "boyishness" of David Letterman's humor should not go unmentioned. Have you ever noticed how frequently he brings up the subject of parents? Of course, there was the great event of "Parents Night," which was a takeoff on those occasions at grade school when parents come squeeze themselves into the kiddy desks and hear what their children have done in math class this semester. Dave figured there was just something intrinsically funny about having everyone's parents turn up to be introduced on camera by their off-spring. And it was in fact a good show, especially when he began to get the parents involved in interacting with his celebrity guest, Howard Cosell (who took the whole strange evening unflappably in his stride), or demonstrating their own talents as singers or magicians.

But that particular evening was by no means the only manifestation of Dave's interest in parents. He has sometimes encouraged celebrities to come on the program with their parents in tow, and may well end up spending more time talking to the parents than to their famous children. Even celebrities who have wisely left mom and dad at home may find that their parents are ultimately part of the evening's entertainment. For example, Henry Winkler was a guest on the show and happened to mention that his father sold redwood siding for a living. Quick as a wink, Dave was on the phone to Winkler *père* to ask his opinion about some problem he was having with the siding on his house in Malibu. When Amy Carter appeared on the show, Dave ended up calling her parents back home in Plains, Georgia, to discuss whether they approved of the outfit she had chosen to wear and other strictly parental questions. It is quite common for him to ask successful entertainers what their parents think about their careers.

In other words, David Letterman proceeds on the assumption that parental approval is an important issue in everyone's life. That attitude seems not only young but almost charmingly dated. In truth, the values of *Late Night with David Letterman* are very close to those of *Happy Days*, or more accurately, to the original 1950s reality on which *Happy Days* is based. Under a thin veneer of contemporary hip, David Letterman is actually treating his audience to a brief visit to a simpler, more innocent time. He doesn't often do jokes about drugs, pregnant teenagers, ideological politics, the arms race, the homeless, AIDS, or any other ugly contemporary reality. He focuses instead on how Paul Shaffer went home to Thunder Bay for Mother's Day, whether anything can be done to pull the Cincinnati Reds out of their season-long slump, what Ron Reagan, Jr.'s parents thought of his appearance on *Saturday Night Live*, how the *Late Night* softball team is faring, and other cozy topics. A regular feature on the show is "Small Town News," Dave's reading of clips from little weekly newspapers about the doings of local inhabitants: the Cherry Pie Bake-Off, police blotter reports of strange behavior, the little triumphs and tragedies that Dave can turn into good comedy. In its own way, *Late Night* itself is rather like those news items: determinedly parochial, eschewing politics and any pursuits that might be classed as intellectual, devoted to gossip rather than analysis.

What *Late Night* and its creators really have in common with the people who live (and report) those small-town news items is a complacent acceptance of the status quo. David Letterman likes to laugh at the things he sees going on around him, but he doesn't *attack* or demand change. His attitude toward television is a perfect example of his position. He likes to make fun of the bad shows on television, and of the pomposity of network executives and self-satisfied celebrities. But he speaks from the position of a person who watches a lot of television, including Jerry Lewis and the *Labor Day Telethon*. If a Kulture Kommittee suddenly swept onto the scene and filled up network television slots with dramatizations of *King Lear* and performances of Mahler symphonies, David Letterman would probably be among the first to complain. He *likes* bad television; it gives him something to laugh about and make fun of.

In the same way that he accepts American television, he also accepts the rest of American society. There's nothing radical about David Letterman. He believes in mom and apple pie and never touching your capital and the American way of life. He makes fun of such things in the way young men have always made fun of their elders. The last thing he'd want to do is tear everything down and replace it with some different ideal. Not only is David Letterman not a radical, he isn't even a member of the counterculture. Contrast his values and attitudes with those conveyed by *Saturday Night Live*, for example, and you'll see the difference. Murray and Belushi and Aykroyd were a genuine part of the counterculture. When they portrayed an "average" family, they did so with the obvious belief that nothing they did in parody could be more ridiculous than the real thing. The Coneheads were no more exotic to the *SNL* crew than Mr. and Mrs. Cleaver. And they always carried around with them the whiff of a life-style that relied on sex and drugs and rock'n'roll—and a fondness for shocking the middle-class world they had rejected.

It's not just David Letterman's preppy jackets and ties that make him stand apart from the guys at *SNL*. For him, the Cleaver family may be funny, but it's also familiar. That way of life is his normalcy, however much he may poke fun at it. Mrs. Cleaver is a lot like his own mom, and he loves his mom and, more significantly, he wants her approval. A little laughter notwithstanding, David Letterman is part of the mainstream of American culture, with solid middle-class values and attitudes. That accounts for his popularity with a mass television audience. It's why he could have been considered (perhaps still is) a suitable replacement for all-American Johnny Carson. He may leave a few scars on a guest every now and again, but he's not threatening the things that viewers really hold dear.

Chapter

12

Comparing the Incomparable

David Letterman is rightly hailed as a creative and original force in television. He has pushed the format of the talk show to include many other elements, such as the remote segments, taped inserts and a type of comedy that is neither stand-up nor sketch. He has used the portability of modern cameras to take viewers all over the NBC building, prowling on the streets of New York, and even flying to Miami. He has made the events of everyday life into television entertainment that often surpasses the carefully rehearsed and choreographed appearances of celebrities. He has been able to make appealing a persona that depends on an unusual mixture of boyishness and cynicism, to deal with pompous celebrities the way the little boy in the crowd dealt with the Emperor Who Had No Clothes, at his best to say the things the audience has been thinking but wouldn't have the nerve to say in public.

But however original David is, he is not the sole creator of all the things he does on the show. In show business, as in every business or profession, people start with some accumulated body of previous experience and then build on it. In David's case, he starts with a long tradition of comic performing and a somewhat briefer tradition of talk show hosting. From these he has selected the elements that make up his own original approach to *Late Night with David Letterman*.

David is quick to acknowledge the influence of others on his comic ideas and performing styles. It was watching Johnny Carson on *Who Do You Trust?* that gave him the idea that you could laugh at ordinary people on a television show and create something that was entertaining without being offensive. It was listening to Arthur Godfrey, and looking at pictures of him snug in his little studio with only his earphones to keep him company, that made Dave see that even a person who is too shy to feel comfortable performing in public can use the airwaves to disseminate his comic ideas. Another influence from the early days was radio personality Rich King, who had a show on WLW in Cincinnati. He used to devote large portions of his program to broadcasting imaginary events, such as paddleboat races on the Ohio River or baseball games between nonexistent teams. Listening to him taught Dave the humorous potential of misinformation. Another early favorite was Jonathan Winters. Dave envied his ability to glean humor from the totally irrelevant. From a later period, Dave credits Jay Leno with demonstrating to him how a comedy routine can be structured so it is more than the sum of its individual jokes.

But of course the most important influences on David Letterman have been the people who do (or have done) more or less what he does himself. His very notion, and ours, of what a talk show is and what a talk show host does came from the people who preceded him in the profession.

Towering head and shoulders over all the rest is of

course Johnny Carson. He has been by far the most successful and by far the best liked of any talk show host. And there's no denying that David learned a lot by watching him, by appearing with him, and by trying to take his place during his stints as guest host on *The Tonight Show*. The similarities between these two men from the Midwest are many and striking. They're both wisecrackers who can quickly defuse the hostility implicit in their snappy remarks by retreating inside their nice-guy personae.

Dave's way of handling segments that aren't a hit with the studio audience is unquestionably modeled after Johnny's. They both comment openly on material that doesn't work. When Johnny is given a pile of pictures with funny captions, or excerpts from schoolchildren's essays, or questions from the audience, and the segment starts to drag, he restlessly mutters about the inadequacy of the material and can be seen to weed through the remaining pieces to try to find something that he thinks is funny. If the segment doesn't start to turn around, he will ask his director if it isn't time to go to a commercial, throw the cards on the floor behind him, or jettison the segment entirely and start to talk to Ed or Doc. Dave behaves much the same way when "Small Town News" or new books from the bookstore or "Viewer Mail" starts to die. The big blue index cards with his lines written on them start to sail around the studio, and he beseeches Hal to know if he isn't out of time now. However, he rarely gives up altogether, perhaps because he is quite skilled at extracting comedy from disaster.

Dave may also have learned from Johnny how to let things go when they start to get out of control. That is one of the things Carson does best, as evidenced by his anthology shows aired every year as an anniversary present to fans. When props don't work or guests get rambunctious, Johnny kicks into overdrive. He shoots off a lot of jokes and does a slow take of incredulity about the whole mess that itself came straight from Jack Benny (and has been handed down to Dave). Johnny tends to paint himself as a victim at such moments, and his victimization is hilarious. Dave follows Johnny's lead and doesn't attempt either to reestablish control of the situation or to gloss over the problem: he sees such incidents as providing the liveliness that he finds missing in a smoothly scheduled show. But this approach to the situation does differ from Johnny's in that Dave is likely to be openly gleeful when foul-ups and unexpected events happen. He's no victim, but an eager participant.

An example of Dave's attitude can be seen in the show on which Andy Kaufman appeared with heavyweight wrestler Jerry Lawler. The two had earlier exchanged insults after participating in a bizarre exhibition match, and as soon as they sat down with Dave, the accusations began flying. Just before a commercial break, Lawler stood up and slapped Kaufman silly, knocking him not just out of his chair but completely off the stage. Shortly after the program resumed, the audience was treated to the sight of Kaufman cursing Lawler and throwing his cup of coffee all over him.

Throughout it all, David Letterman was all but gloating over the melee. He made jokes aplenty, and took the attitude that viewers of network television were really in for a treat. His off-the-cuff responses made the whole thing so funny that NBC agreed to air the show with the fight scenes intact (although some of Andy Kaufman's language was bleeped to protect innocent ears). Later it emerged that the fight was in fact a put-up job, agreed upon by Lawler and Kaufman before they took to the air, and that caused a flurry of statements from NBC and *Late Night* about how they had not been a party to the plans. Dave himself joked, "Some of these words are okay to say on TV but one should not throw coffee. I've said it a thousand times." But whether or not it was planned in advance by the principals, it was still one of Dave's finest hours, and a perfect example of the way he can handle the unexpected and make it funny.

Looking at the ways David Letterman *differs* from Johnny Carson is also instructive. Johnny wears the mantle of stardom very comfortably. He is invariably dapperly tailored, wearing clothes that make him look like an executive on his way to the country club; his silver hair is always exactly the right length. David gives the impression that he can't wait to rip off his tie; Johnny seems to have been born in his. Johnny is obviously a part of show business (although he manages to keep his ego under control). When he talks about glamorous events in Tinseltown, you assume he was a participant. You assume David just saw it on *Entertainment Tonight* like the rest of us. Johnny makes it seem that his celebrity guests are also his friends, whereas David makes them seem like paid professional entertainers doing a turn. Johnny makes it all look easy, but David makes it all look improbable. "What kind of a show are we running?" he likes to ask the heavens as yet another strange guest waits in the wings.

Johnny Carson may be the most obvious person to compare David Letterman with, but he's not the most significant. You learn more about the way David Letterman works as a performer by comparing him with another host of *The Tonight Show*: Steve Allen.

Steve was the guy who originated the show, back in 1954, when NBC had nothing yet but a ninety-minute time slot, a New York studio, and a catchy title. He was the one who created the format and pioneered some of its elements. According to Steve, "For the first three years, it was not a talk show but an experimental laboratory. I had almost total freedom to do any damn thing I wanted to. One night we might book the Basie band, another night a debate about the blacklist, followed by a guest appearance of the Harlem Globetrotters." Part of the reason this eclectic collection worked was that it accurately mirrored the interests of its multifaceted host. Steve Allen is the author of scores of books (he once hosted a radio program called *Hooked on Books*), an inveterate collector of trivia, a supporter of many charitable and humanitarian causes. He has written more than 4,000 songs, among them several standards such as "Impossible" and "This Could Be the Start of Something Big." He has published poetry, including a collection of verse published under the pseudonym of William Christopher Stevens, allegedly "one of Australia's best-known poets," that drew respectful response from reviewers before it was revealed as an Allen hoax. "It kills me that someday I'll have to die," he says despairingly. "I don't see how I'll ever get it all done."

Steve spoke in a 1974 interview for *Television Quarterly* about what he thought made his version of a talk show special. "There's no doubt that *musically* the original show was head and shoulders over anything around today. After all, our four original singers were Eydie Gorme, Pat Kirby, Steve Lawrence and Andy Williams. Today none of the shows even have regular singers. Doc Severinsen and Bobby Rosengarden played in Skitch Henderson's house band [on Steve's show]. And—since I'm a musician—music in general, including the booking of artists from jazz to opera, was much more important when I ran the show."

Allen made an interesting distinction between the original *Tonight Show* and its descendants. "My version of *The Tonight Show*—strictly speaking—was a comedy program, not a talk show. It was quite different from the

comedy formula of *Broadway Open House* but, at the other
extreme, it was not the Griffin-Cavett-Carson idea of just
propping up four or five people on a couch and talking
to them one at a time. The couch was really invented by
Jack Paar. I used the Talk Show element as a building-
block of the program, but it was only one of several. We
did a great many sketches, a great many character monologues, booked a lot more comedians than they do now.
People like Jonathan Winters, Louis Nye, Don Knotts,
Mort Sahl and other new comics of the 1950s were frequent visitors."

As the host of *The Tonight Show*, Steve Allen was a
brilliant ad-libber. He was able to draw on not just his
comedic talent but also a wide range of information suitable for almost any occasion. He was notably quick to
take his comedy where he found it: in the behavior of a
guest, the script of some announcement he was supposed
to read, the misadventures of some carefully prepared
sketch. As he put it, "I always manage to see something
ridiculous in whatever matter I have under consideration."

For his part, Steve has expressed his admiration for
David Letterman. "If the world came to me and asked
whether David Letterman should be on television for thirty-
five years, I would vote yes on that. I think he will last
because, for one thing, he's—to use that old-fashioned
expression—easygoing. He doesn't wear you out. Some
people have asked me, 'Well, don't you think he's a little
arch?' And I say, 'Not for my taste. I dig him.' But I know
what they're talking about. It could be that it's just going
to take people a while to get used to his style." When
told that many people consider Letterman his descendant,
if not successor, he replies, "I'm complimented anyone
would think that. A lot of comedians in David's age bracket
used to watch me, but I think whoever you watch in your

ultimate field of endeavor when you're fourteen is going to be an influence."

All the people at *Late Night* are frank in admitting that Steve Allen was a major influence on the way their show was conceived. Although they are not specific about the way they used the model of Steve's *Tonight Show*, careful observation can turn up the similarities. One of the most important is the use of ordinary citizens as a source of comedy. "We used to go into the audience and put cameras outside for remote bits," agrees Steve. One journalist described it: "Ten minutes of each show was devoted to the street scene outside the studio: an old lady hobbling, a fire engine racing away, a derelict angrily giving the camera the finger, and after the first night, several would-be TV stars 'auditioning' dance or pantomime or naïvely holding signs with their names on them." Dave sometimes uses similar footage of miscellaneous passersby, but he'll narrate the footage and call it "New York's February 8 Day Parade." But Steve also hedged by using comic actors as well. His "Man in the Street" features frequently relied on the talents of his resident troupe of comics, such as Louis Nye, Don Knotts, and Tom Poston; they were all skilled in responding to his questions as if they were ordinary people who had been dragged blinking and shuffling in front of the camera and had nothing whatsoever to say. Dave has omitted the "ringers" and stuck with the concept of the ordinary person as funny, without prepared scripts or coaching. The risks are bigger that way, but so too may be the payoff.

Steve Allen liked found humor and low-budget jokes. He would create a big fanfare about giving out some award, which turned out to be a giant salami from Katz's delicatessen. His guests included such oddities as a chicken impersonator, a ten-year-old columnist writing advice to the kiddie lovelorn, and Lenny Bruce in his only national television exposure. Instead of "Small Town News," Steve read aloud Letters to the Editor printed in the *New York Daily News*, mercilessly exposing the attitudes of the writers.

Another influence of Steve Allen can be seen in the almost surrealistic "sight gags" that Steve used to do and Dave continues to feature on *Late Night*. Letterman fans all recall the time he was covered in Alka-Seltzer tablets and lowered into a vat of water to make a giant headache remedy. But were they aware that Steve Allen had pioneered that type of humor? Steve had himself covered with tea bags and then dunked in a tub of hot water, to brew a huge cup of tea. Like Dave, he found incongruities of size inherently funny and took a lively interest in people who claimed to have the Biggest Whatever.

Steve also liked to talk about *The Tonight Show* as if it were some sort of amateur, low-budget production, just the way Dave talks about *Late Night*. On one of the first broadcasts of the show, Steve warned, "This is not going to be an Extravaganza. It'll be more of a Monotonous." That's a joke that could fit right into David Letterman's mouth. Steve also derived a great deal of humor from things on the show that went wrong: the props that failed, the mistakes made by the crew, the flubs that inevitably came from doing a ninety-minute show five times a week. In fact, he still likes to stress the imperfection of those broadcasts. Looking back on the show, he commented, "These glowing tributes to the *Tonight Show* of the 1950s are, I think, written by people who are remembering only the peak moments and forgetting that on many a night the show came under the heading of 'What-else-is-new?' " And he clearly appreciates the amateur element of *Late Night*. Interviewed by Charles M. Young on the set of *Late Night* just before he was appearing as a guest on the show, Steve made a big point about how there was no one around to help him with his toupee. "They had no hairdresser, so they're sending out for a gardener," he cracked. "It's supposed to go back here," he indicated dubiously, "but if you have any other ideas, just pitch in." No doubt it pleased him to be on a show that proudly announces it's the only show on television that uses no hairspray.

Steve also started the tradition of interacting with the audience, one that both Johnny Carson and David Letterman have followed. Steve's audience was better behaved; there was none of that catcalling and jeering that *Late Night* studio audiences indulge in. But he did talk directly to them, ask their opinion about what was going on, incorporate some of their audible comments, and occasionally encourage them to mayhem. Dave's physical interaction with the audience is fairly limited. He doesn't often go out into the seats and talk to members of the audience, and when he does, he maintains a certain emotional distance. But he interacts with them verbally all through the show, chiding them for their responses, pleading for their understanding ("I'm just a kid trying to make a living . . . leave me alone, will you?") and cracking up over the jokes they shout to him. His rapport with the studio audience is so strong that sometimes he forgets that three or four million other people are watching and goes on with jokes that were obviously initiated during the warm-up, before the cameras started to roll, that only he and the people in the studio can appreciate.

Unlike most stars, Dave warms up his own audience (with a little help from Bill Wendell). When asked why he does it himself, he shoots back, "Just in case they're all from Portugal and don't speak a word of English I want to be the first to know." More seriously, he continues, "I like to know where the audience is. Are they up? Down? Are they mostly tourists? People from out of town are generally a bit more sedate than New Yorkers. This warm-up is really more for me than for the audience. It's like batting practice. And then, as I'm walking away from the audience, I have a clear, preconceived notion of how the show will go."

David Letterman's on-the-air personality has many similarities to Steve Allen's. Both men seem a bit restless, impatient, quickly bored when things are running along too smoothly. Both subtly convey a sense of superiority in comparison with the ordinary; Steve too induces his audience to join him in laughing gently at the foibles of others. Moreover, they share a kind of elitism in their attitude toward the rest of television, a secret conviction that theirs is about the only show worth watching. And both seem like personally shy men who are ill at ease when performing live. Steve Allen's wife, actress Jayne Meadows, tells a story about how she first met him that confirms he is an essentially shy creature. "He sat down beside me [at a dinner party] and said not one word to me. At the end of the evening, I turned and said, 'Mr. Allen, you're either the rudest man I've ever met or the shyest.' His face turned red and he slumped, and I had my answer. He was shy."

Once again, however, the differences are as illuminating as the similarities. Steve Allen is a genuine intellectual, a man whose ultimate idea of real entertainment was expressed in his PBS series *Meeting of Minds*, a show that featured actors impersonating great historical figures such as Plato, Isaac Newton, and Martin Luther. They were thrown together in a talk show format, discussing the great ideas of Western civilization. David Letterman, on the other hand, is the kind of man who has trouble pronouncing "ophthalmologist" and makes a point of letting you know the fact. He is quick-thinking but not especially knowledgeable; he may know Buddy Biancalana's batting average but isn't likely to volunteer many hard facts about the Italian Renaissance.

David Letterman's approach to comedy *is*, however, cerebral. His jokes, for example, require listeners to supply the context that makes them funny. They are sometimes conceptual, with the humor coming from an unexpected juxtaposition of realities. They are often verbal; for example, the way he likes to play around with people's names, or his amusement over the way some words sound, like "Guam." But he is not an intellectual person, and his humor is not intellectual humor. He's not interested in ideas or concepts; he's not trying to broadcast any heavy message. He's just a bright, observant person looking out at the world around him and perceiving its innate humor.

Another difference between the two talk show hosts is that Steve Allen has a real interest in politics. Although he claims that he didn't become a political creature until he was past thirty, Allen used his celebrity, and often his air time, to promote causes he believed in: the plight of the migrant workers, the dangers of the arms race, the obligation to extend civil rights to all minorities, the needs of the poor and homeless. And when he was attacked for airing his views, he simply became more outspoken. "I wouldn't have been surprised to receive those letters from a mental institution," he reflected, "but they were from people walking the streets." David Letterman, however, is determinedly apolitical. He rarely tells jokes about politics of any sort, and he confesses that he is not even registered to vote. When political humor is injected into *Late Night*, it usually doesn't come out of the mouth of David Letterman, but from Bill Wendell, the announcer. For example, Bill has introduced Dave as "the man who feels that if we give $100 million to the Contras, we'd better damn well get a receipt"—not exactly sharp political satire, but one of the few times a subject such as aid to the Contras has even been mentioned on the program. Apparently Dave and his writers agree that even mildly political jokes are not for him personally. Where Steve Allen used jokes to attack the status quo, and even Johnny Carson often incorporates biting antigovernment jokes, Dave stays away from issue-oriented humor of any sort.

One exception to the general lack of political interest on *Late Night*, which presumably reflects similar sentiments on the part of its predominantly eighteen-to-thirty-four-year-old audience, is a tendency to mention municipal problems in New York City. Problems with the transportation system, threatened strikes, scandal in high places, and of course, the revelations about corruption within the city bureaucracy are all grist for David Letterman's mill. He learned to do that sort of local humor back home in Indiana, and it still strikes him as funny. And these stories about problems in New York are not essentially political in nature. They are more like "tall tales" of the city, an old tradition of joke and story telling. They could almost be set up in that old vaudevillian style:

A: Things are really bad in my city.
B: How bad are they?
A: They're so bad that they're holding old-fashioned two-for-one public official bribe days.
B: That's nothing. In my town, things are so bad that . . .

Instead, the joke is simply put in the mouth of Bill Wendell: "And now, from New York, home of the old-fashioned, two-for-one public official bribe days . . ." and so on.

That leads to one other very significant difference between the humor of Steve Allen and that of David Letterman. Many critics have commented that Steve Allen has the soul of an anarchist. He tells sharp political jokes because he believes that in many ways the social and political system of America stinks. He is keenly aware of the unfairness, the prejudice, the way the haves avert their gaze from the have-nots. Personally, he is a sober and thoughtful man who manages without being stuffy to have some very strong opinions about the ills of our society. And although he is happily married and has fathered four children, you get the impression that he regards social conventions as so much hooey. He's not only iconoclastic, but he seems genuinely undisturbed by other people's opinions of his opinions. When asked if it bothers him to hear the unflattering way he is sometimes labeled by others, he answered lightly, "They can call me a hockey puck for all I care."

This is in direct contrast to David Letterman, who laughs at but nevertheless accepts the way things are. Himself a decent and honorable man, he remains undisturbed by the specter of social, political, or economic inequity. He does admit to an interest in knowing how much money people earn for various jobs, a question he frequently pops to his guests. "I just think people find it interesting to know. I do." He goes on to comment, "Hell, I'm terribly overpaid—and Carson makes twelve times more. It's tough for an assembly-line guy to swallow that." But, in Dave's basically accepting view, it's tough mostly because that guy isn't on the long end of the stick—not because all the sticks should be the same length. This easy acceptance is no doubt related to his success in a mass medium: reformers are notably boring company. And although he is as of this writing neither married nor a father, he obviously accepts the social conventions of both states with equanimity. Moreover, it is clear that it *does* matter to David Letterman what people think of him, at least in some regards. It is important to him not to seem to be a jerk, or a fool, or a pompous celebrity.

Another early television pioneer to whom David Letterman is sometimes compared is Ernie Kovacs. For those who missed the work of this original and inventive comedian, Kovacs appeared on various television shows between 1950 and his tragic death in 1962, at the age of forty-two. He was never a real commercial success and had to struggle to find a forum during his lifetime. In the decades since his death, more and more people are recognizing what a debt television comedy owes Kovacs; and colleges, museums, and public broadcasting stations continue to sponsor retrospective showings of his work.

In the 1950s, when Steve Allen was host of *The Tonight Show*, Ernie Kovacs was a regular guest host. In Ernie's hands, the show was full of surprises. When a celebrity guest proved to be dull and Ernie deduced that the interview had gone as far as it could, he simply counted down the last sixty seconds until the scheduled time slot was over. When he emerged on the set, full of caricatured geniality, he addressed the viewers: "Thank you for letting us into your living room. But couldn't you have cleaned up a little?" Coming back after a commercial break, he looked straight into the camera and said, "There is a purpose to this program, although it may not appear to the naked eye." Like David Letterman, Ernie Kovacs had lived through the frustrating experience of having a show canceled. Unlike Dave, he did not try to keep a stiff upper lip. He devoted his last show on the air to dismantling the set with an ax.

Kovacs was especially inventive in the way he used the technology of television; as one critic put it, "He treated TV as if he owned it." He realized that television opened up new possibilities never before available to comedians.

He once said, "It is not photographed vaudeville. Television is unique, it is across the room, it's on a little box." He experimented endlessly. He got the cameras to move with him, to view the scene from an unexpected point of view; once he even taped a kaleidoscope to the lens to create a fragmented visual image. He used blackouts, cutaways, and other gimmicks in ways that made comments on the material he was performing. Shows such as *Rowan and Martin's Laugh-In*, *Saturday Night Live*, and *Monty Python's Flying Circus* have adapted this use of bizarre juxtapositions and apparently unrelated sketches that turn out to have similar themes, or lines, or visual images that tie them together. Kovacs liked to show the audience what the camera could do. For example, in one segment, he attempted to educate his audience on the formula for success in Hollywood: "Beat it to death." To demonstrate, he showed the audience a gunfight shot from half a dozen different camera angles, including one through the bullethole left in the loser. In one sketch, he himself looked fuzzy and distorted, but he warned the audience, "There's nothing wrong with your sets; I'm just slow to focus."

Today, critics call what Ernie Kovacs did back in the 1950s "art." Sometimes his art reminded you of Saul Steinberg; for example, when he drew a bold black line on the floor, then made the line oscillate like a radio wave and turn into the music from "Mack the Knife." On other occasions, his art was more like Magritte: a man holds a candle, then walks out of the screen, leaving behind the flame. Sometimes his images were surreal: a painting of a lake suddenly bursts a dam and water pours out of the wall, or he opens a copy of *Camille* and hears a cough. Critic Ross Wetzsteon, writing in the *Village Voice*, commented, "If Dali hadn't imagined a melting watch, Kovacs surely would have."

What made Ernie Kovacs especially appealing is that

he didn't take himself seriously. He never made claims for himself as an artist; instead he told his wife, "Oh, who the hell is watching anyway? Put it on!" He described the medium of television as "an intimate void," and he often went out of his way to emphasize the temporary nature of his work. For example, he would spend a very large budget for a very short segment. One of his funniest moments came when, as a high-pressure car salesman, he patted the fender of the lemon he was trying to hawk and the whole thing fell through the floor. That gag cost more than $13,000 to shoot and was over in approximately three seconds—one reason he found it hard to win a regular slot with a national sponsor. Wetzsteon, writing in the *Village Voice*, expounded, "That car plunging through the floor is priceless anarchy. Such audacity doesn't tickle us into laughter, it stuns. Another comic would have had the car itself collapse, satirizing the shoddiness of the product by slightly exaggerating our expectation; but by having the very floor collapse, Kovacs was getting a laugh out of the instability of the world, utterly *shattering* our expectations."

Certainly, some of his comments about television are reminiscent of David Letterman's attitude of "what the hell, it's only network TV." And both men share an interest in demystifying their medium. In a bit on a 1951 show, Ernie hung a cardboard control panel over his chest, used his face as a picture tube, and instructed his viewers on how to adjust the knobs for vertical and horizontal hold. In another show made that same year, he had the camera follow him as he strolled down the studio corridor to the water fountain to get a drink. He liked to use props that were obviously fake; for example, he had a skit about the "Colossal Cowboy" (Ernie in a cowboy suit) who is stepping on little model towns that are the ultimate in sleazy unconvincing fakery. His dancing or classical-music-playing gorillas were always wearing cheap dime-store gorilla masks like kids wear on Halloween rather than the realistic Hollywood props he could have used. On one of his shows, the final credits proudly proclaimed, "A Production of an El Cheapo Subsidiary."

David Letterman has certainly adopted Ernie's attitude and revels in cheap props and unconvincing effects. For example, when the American Museum of Natural History lent him a plaster replica of a Neanderthal skull, he took joy in pointing out that it probably cost no more than $5, was only six months old, and was completely fake. He emphasized the point by rigging the skull up to spit water through its teeth, emit puffs of smoke, and eventually to ride around the studio floor on a little remote-controlled sled, which toppled over every time Dave tried to take the skull around a curve. He loved every minute of such failures.

One of *Late Night*'s staff writers explained that they like to do "conceptual" humor, and that points out another similarity to the work of Ernie Kovacs. The shifts of context that are a Letterman specialty are actually very close to some of Kovacs' surrealism. Asking Mariel Hemingway to come on the program and clean fish, or the obscure entertainer Pearl Burnett to sing "When Irish Eyes Are Smiling" as she shreds a giant piece of paper to make a replica of an Irish lace tablecloth, or asking Larry "Bud" Melman to do just about anything, obviously classifies as conceptual art. It's not the actions themselves that are entertaining (God knows!) or even inherently interesting; it's the context of network television, the very notion that such stuff could be shown on it, that makes such activities entertaining. Or makes them art. Or makes them just plain unbelievable! In other words, you have to think about it before you find it amusing—that's conceptual humor. It's light-years away from old-fashioned one-liners or physical comedy like slipping on a banana peel.

Another way that David Letterman is similar to Ernie Kovacs is their shared ability to make their own viewers feel culturally superior to viewers of other television programs. In a sense, it's biting the hand that feeds you: you get a television program and appear in front of a mass television audience to talk about the stupidity of watching television, or at least everyone else's version of it. David Letterman once gave some hints about how this balancing act works. "Even though I have a rather large ego—anyone who goes into comedy has a bottomless ego—I still feel more comfortable in a not fully accepted circumstance than I do if I'm surrounded and engulfed and embraced. I always felt better being a little on the outside in high school, kind of lobbing in annoying things from the outer periphery. It's just easier to be on the outside making fun of it. This show is a little fortress, a little bastion, from which I can whine about practically anything. We're just an irritant. We're like a gnat trying to sink *The Love Boat*."

When Dave says things like, "Gee, I might as well sell my VCR; they're canceling *Benson, Different Strokes* and *The Love Boat*," he is allowing his viewers to feel superior to the television culture, while still participating in it fully. That ambivalence was pioneered by Ernie Kovacs. He loved to attack the low level of television fare; as critic Jeff Greenfield put it, "He found in the treacle of broadcasting an irresistible target of opportunity." But at the same time, his own highest ambition was to have a regular show on television.

Another similarity is that both men come across as smart without being in the least intellectual. Ross Wetzsteon said about Ernie Kovacs, "He only gave the impression of intelligence, and when he expressed 'ideas' in his work, they were the 'ideas' of a bright skeptical adolescent. Television artists had no larger vision—the vantage point from which they skewered mass culture was from within mass culture itself." These words apply equally well to David Letterman. He too is "bright" without having any special interest in the world of ideas. And he is similarly limited in his perspective, which comes primarily from years of exposure to mass media. This is in direct contrast to someone like Steve Allen, who could be part of the mass media culture but also had the ability to step outside that culture and view it from a different vantage point, the world of books and ideas. David Letterman's references are all from TV's mass culture: we laugh because, like him, we are familiar with the original version— not so much a specific television show, or even a specific person on television, but the cumulative effect of years of listening to late-night announcers extoll the merits of Ginsu knives and bamboo steamers; of overwrought game-show hosts building up almost entirely fictitious big moments out of ordinary people's confusion; of the kind of hyperbole that keeps shows like *Entertainment Tonight* and *Lifestyles of the Rich and Famous* on the air. *Late Night* is one big inside joke.

But in many key ways, David Letterman is very different from Ernie Kovacs. Perhaps most significantly this is so because Kovacs' humor is almost entirely visual, whereas David's is heavily verbal, springing from an enjoyment of the sound of words and an awareness of the way their meanings can be manipulated. David likes words as symbols, and also as objects of humor in themselves, but Ernie Kovacs had little interest in words for any purpose. Most of his best segments are either completely silent or performed to music.

Another important difference is the use of the studio audience. Kovacs, in most of his comedy shows, had none. As Chevy Chase pointed out, "Without the input from a live audience, it is difficult for a comedian to gauge the effects of his rhythms and timing accurately. In certain pieces, it tended to make Ernie run long. But at least he had the courage, originality and integrity to go with his own comic instincts." That lack of an audience helped Kovacs create his own private world, but it also tended to seal him hermetically inside it. As a viewer, you almost feel like a Peeping Tom; Kovacs is so obviously doing what he does for himself rather than for the benefit of the viewers.

David Letterman, on the other hand, really depends on his studio audiences. "Those 250 people are the only indication I have of what is funny. If they don't laugh, we're doing something wrong." Dave plays to that audience, and they are warm in their encouragement of his special brand of comedy. He often addresses them directly: "My oh my, what a handsome group of humans we've assembled here tonight. How many of you are having the time of your life?" Don't make the mistake of thinking they are tourists who were collared as they walked along Sixth Avenue looking for the way to get back to their hotel. In fact, tickets to the *Late Night* studio audience are hard to come by. One must write NBC to ask for them, and then wait for a reply. And when the coveted tickets do arrive, they will probably be for a night two or three months in the future—that's how big the demand is. Thus the studio audience functions like a David Letterman Fan Club, packed with people who know and love him. That certainly makes him more comfortable, which in turn helps him to relax and ad-lib as freely as if he was just sitting around with a group of friends. It does also mean, however, that he frequently plays to the studio audience, and eventually that becomes a kind of limitation too.

Another significant difference is the level of manic behavior in Kovacs' work, which is more or less non-existent on *Late Night*. Kovacs not only did visual and physical comedy, he often did it at high speed, and in a deliberately crazy way. About the only way to see his work today is through the anthology shows that have been put together as special tributes, and they all suffer from the problem of disrupting the original Kovacs pace. Although he was not afraid to let the camera linger on him as he stared into it, or slowly, sloooowly changed from one expression to another, the salient characteristic of much of his work, as it originally appeared, was a truly dizzying pace, highly varied and full of funny juxtapositions. This may in large part explain why he was never successful in a regularly slotted show: no one but Ernie Kovacs could stand the pace for long. There was too much to see, too much to think about. Audiences were still processing the last joke but one while Ernie was forging on to something completely different.

David Letterman is in this respect much better company. He never rushes his material, and he is not a frenetic personality. He takes it easy as a host, with the result that the audience, too, feels relaxed. If a segment is going well, he will let it run overtime. For example, a feature using the Super Slo-Mo camera showed no signs of haste or pressure, even when some of the props didn't work as expected. The grand finale, which featured a heavy-duty bear trap and many balloons filled with pudding, required innumerable takes before David could get the balloons to hit and trigger the bear trap to produce the satisfying squish everyone was waiting for. But Dave took it easy, made jokes with the audience, eventually threw one of the pudding-filled balloons out to a group of guys (one of whom promptly threw it back to him, creating a situation that very nearly led to a pudding-covered host). Dave's casual attitude, and his ability to get just as much out of things that don't work as those that do, make him very easy to be with four nights a week. One critic has pointed out that he is actually even more relaxed than Johnny Carson, who can be observed to squirm and sweat when jokes fail or skits go wrong. As long as David Letterman can keep himself out of a situation in which he appears to be trying too hard, he sails along without ever causing us to worry for his sake. In the event of a failed joke, or a nonworking prop, or a totally recalcitrant guest, Dave just comments, "This whole show is cursed," or says coolly, "I'll just take my own life one of these days, and you'll know why." For the most part, he's unflappable (as long as no one mentions sex). Where Ernie Kovacs fit media theorist Marshall McLuhan's definition of "hot," meaning well defined, larger than life, coming on strong, David Letterman is the perfect embodiment of McLuhan's "cool," a bit remote, detached, never pressing too hard, allowing viewers to fill in the spaces with their own interpretations, feelings, responses. According to McLuhan, by the way, "cool" is what works best on the medium of television.

One of the most illuminating comparisons to make with David Letterman is a broadcasting personality who was almost certainly not a personal influence on Dave, nor vice versa. Instead, it seems to be a case of parallel development: one that tells us a lot about the midwestern ethos. The broadcaster in question is Garrison Keillor, host and star of *A Prairie Home Companion*, which originates in Minneapolis and is carried by the PBS radio network. Keillor's format is quite different, a weekly two-hour show, with a guest list limited to performing musicians. It's an idiosyncratic variety show, featuring advertisements for imaginary products such as Powdermilk Biscuits ("Heavens, they're tasty") and Raw Bits, the cereal that demands to know whether you're man enough to eat it. The musicians on the show function as a kind of repertory company, reading some of the commercial spots and doing short skits with Garrison. For many fans, the highlight of the show is Garrison's monologue about the news from back home in Lake Wobegon, the little town that time forgot and the decades cannot improve. By turns riotously funny, shrewdly observational, and heart-tuggingly emotional, the monologues are above all else the ruminations of a humane and mature spirit.

Like Dave, Garrison likes to use highfalutin hyperbole to point out the gap between expectation and reality. He too "quotes" those old-fashioned announcers and their desperate enthusiasm, in a way that makes us laugh at the pretensions of advertising hype and at ourselves for often falling for it. He also delights in the reverse of the coin, the deliberately underplayed event (or commercial). For example, one of his imaginary sponsors is Ralph's Pretty Good Grocery, the store that reminds you that if you can't find it at Ralph's, you can probably get along without it. And Garrison too is always interested in the media as a topic of humor, ranging from mild cracks to almost criminally funny satire. For weeks in 1985, at the time that Ted Turner was threatening to take over CBS, Garrison had a running bit about how his father had bought him CBS. Week after week, he discussed what he planned to do with it, and explained the obstacles to progress. It amounted to a crash course in media baiting.

Garrison's sense of humor overlaps with Dave's in many respects. They both like the positively silly and grotesque. For Dave, it's the fly feeder, which you fill with carrion or rotting fruit to attract flies to your porch; for Garrison, it's the company that offers chicken-feather siding, an attractive and durable way to cover ugly stucco, brick, or even aluminum siding on your house. They are

both very verbal comedians. Dave reaches for his Cup O'
Coffee and his Bag o' Bees. Garrison advertises the Fear
Monger Shop in "the Dales," which turn out to include
Chippendale, Airedale, Clydesdale, and Mondale. Dave
books Alba Ballard, the woman who dresses up parrots
like celebrities, and Dave Bender's talking birds to entertain his audience; Garrison doesn't have to book the real
birds but can do his monologue about a pair of traveling
revivalists who appear with their Gospel Birds, who have
been trained to fly into the audience and take up the
collection.

More significant than the similarities in their sense of
humor are the similarities in their points of view. Garrison
Keillor's monologues reveal a set of values very like those
that underlie David Letterman's jokes and comments. Each
is a small-town Midwesterner who honors his father and
mother, hasn't told a lie since childhood, and feels it is
unseemly to attract too much attention to oneself. They
have both fought against being "changed" by success,
and have somehow found the secret to keeping the small-
town boy in themselves alive and well, despite being
featured in *Time* or *Newsweek* and adored by millions of
fans. Both men are in fact the heirs of a long tradition in
American humor: the country boy who goes to the big
city and, while appearing to be immensely impressed by
the greater knowledge and sophistication of the city dwell-
ers, actually displays greater wisdom and understanding
than they do. Mark Twain wrote about heroes like this,
and Will Rogers was a famous embodiment of the type,
whose just-plain-cowboy persona cloaked a shrewdly critical intelligence. Garrison Keillor is the boy from Lake
Wobegon who remains forever impressed by the dazzle-
ment of Minneapolis-St. Paul; heck, he's even impressed
by St. Cloud! David Letterman reminds us that even a
midwestern city like Indianapolis is really just a conjunc-

tion of small towns and thus portrays himself as a small-town boy who is bemused by the big city in which he finds himself. Like Herb Shriner before him, he capitalizes on the Hoosier image.

Both Garrison and Dave are using an aspect of their personalities that is real. They really are the people you get to know through their shows. Dave's friend Jay Leno says, "There's no hypocrisy in what he does. What you see is what's there. I think he tends to lead his life exactly the way he behaves on television. He's not at all phony. He has the amazing ability to be a professional performer who reacts to situations in a way that corresponds with how people at home probably would." Yet it isn't quite that simple. David Letterman is the one out of a million who became a star, and he's different from the people at home. His talent is in being able to represent what they think, but do it in a way that has insight and humor. Perhaps he speaks for many people in the audience when he confronts Don King and asks bluntly about why his hair looks so odd. But only Dave knows how to get the comedy out of the confrontation, how to make it something more than merely embarrassing.

Dave has talked about how he has learned to "be himself" on a television show watched by millions of people. "In the beginning, I thought the closer to your actual self you were on the show, the better it would be. But now, having done it for three years and a couple of months, I realize you definitely have to be more than yourself. You have to pretend that you're bigger than you are, that you're enjoying it more than you really are. It all has to be blown up. . . ." In other words, you start out with the person you really are and then you use it. That's the fundamental process of art, whether you use it to write a novel, paint a picture, or create a comic persona to star on a television show. Dave has taken his genuine Hoosier heritage and turned it into something more. People identify with Dave, to the extent that he does represent attitudes and values that are common to middle America. But they also recognize that he does more than merely represent their attitudes. He also transfigures them, and turns them into a very entertaining form of art.

Chapter

13

Whither
David Letterman?

It makes David Letterman uneasy to admit that he is a success.

"Success in show business?" he cracks. "That's someone like Michael Jackson." Faced with the irrefutable fact that his ratings went up by 25 percent in his third year on the air, he muses, "I don't know what the hell happened. We're not doing anything different on the show. Actually, I thought we were doing better shows in some ways in our first and second years. Maybe we've just worn people down. They just say, 'Oh, alright, oh God, we'll watch your damned show.' " He concludes with a thought that seems to give him some comfort. "The ratings'll probably just go back down again."

That's possible, but most observers agree it's not likely. David has clearly found his audience, and it seems likely that they will prove loyal: a group of cultists, even if they don't exactly live outside Yuma eating road kill. The devotion is manifest not just in the ratings, and those desirable demographics, but in the actions of the fans themselves. If you talk to a studio audience as they are filing in, you will quickly learn that many of them are repeat visitors, some embarking on their fifteenth or twenty-third return trip to see their hero live. And the fans are incredibly knowledgeable. They can remember word for word things David said, not just in the first season of *Late Night* but even back on the old morning show. (No doubt they will soon be writing in with their lists of inaccuracies in this book.) Those who can produce their ticket stubs to prove they were in the studio audience for the morning show are almost cult idols themselves. Like garrulous elders who pass along the oral history of the clan, they tell more-recent fans what it was really like in the old days.

Not even David Letterman can ignore the reality of such success. What he wants to do with it is another question. He has said more than once that he'd like to see *Late Night* stay on the air long enough to become an accepted ritual in Televisionland. The impression that counts, he thinks, is the one he makes over the long haul. A good show one night, a mediocre show the next: it's not the specifics that matter but the overall impression left by weeks, months, even years of viewing. That's certainly been true of Johnny Carson. Even the frequent anniversary shows that dredge up clips from previous years and attempt to anthologize *The Tonight Show* don't really explain why America loves Johnny Carson. It's not those highlights, or any others. It's the constant companionship of more than twenty years, the ever-increasing familiarity with his attitudes, his reactions, his expressions, his personality—that's the key to his place in the annals of television.

Dave has pointed out how being on television really boils down to exhibiting your personality to millions of people in the hope it will please them. "What you're doing is saying to a group of strangers, 'Here are some things that I find amusing and here is my personality. I would like you to respond by laughing.' They may think, 'We like it okay, but we're not going to laugh.' If that's the case, you're going to think about loading a cheap revolver and taking your own life." And he rightly adds that merely pleasing 80 percent of the audience is not enough. In show business, it's either total success, with the entire audience laughing, or it's equivalent to total failure.

The verdict of the viewers seems to be that David Letterman has a personality that is easy to be with and a sense of humor that they can share. He no longer stuns us with the unexpected, nor do his asides very often sail right past us. We have learned to understand the way he sees things, and to a great extent to share in that vision. The influence of *Late Night* is pervasive, especially among the younger people who make up the typical viewership. Not only do you see outright imitations of David Letterman being done by comics all over the country (Joe Piscopo, by the way, does an especially good Letterman), but his style of humor and type of delivery can be heard in the routines of younger comics and in the banter of college students on college campuses everywhere. Unquestionably, he is beginning to achieve the success he wanted, in shaping the way millions of people perceive the humor of everyday life.

But does he really want to emulate Johnny Carson and stay on the air, doing essentially the same thing over and over for twenty more years? Remember that David Letterman is a person who is easily bored. Establishing the show, creating a format that would work for him, finding the right people to collaborate with him on the air and behind the scenes, learning to improve his interviewing skills, relaxing on the air to achieve a more intimate communication with his viewers, devising ways to use the technology of television to show viewers how a show is really put on the air: all these were challenges that David rose to in the first few years that the show was on the air. But somehow it's hard to imagine him doing it throughout the coming decades, growing white-haired before our collective eyes, ending up as a beloved senior citizen of the show business community with a record for longevity even better than Dick Clark's.

The truth of the matter is that *Late Night* is presently on the verge of turning into exactly the sort of television show that David Letterman doesn't like: a sampler of well-recognized pieces of material that evoke automatic laughter even before the audience hears them performed. There's "Stupid Pet Tricks," and "Viewer Mail," and a "Brush with Greatness," and phone calls Dave will make for you, and the "Hard to Believe," and etiquette for various daily occurrences, and the "Top Ten Lists," and so on and so on; every fan knows what to expect already. Then the banter with Paul, the taped remotes with funny reports from various businesses in New York, even the breaking glass as Dave tosses his cards through what looks like a window. . . . They make the show popular, and they make it recognizable. But they also trap David Letterman within their confines. Answer frankly: when was the last time you saw something really unexpected on the show? Now answer frankly: do you think David Letterman will enjoy doing that stuff just that way for the next twenty years?

One way to think about the answer to that question is to try to imagine what he might be doing instead. Of course, one possibility that has recently sparked a new round of speculation is that he might "take over" Johnny Carson's show when Johnny finally decides to retire. During the years when Joan Rivers was Johnny's official guest host, Dave had a brief respite from the questions about whether or not he might be Johnny's replacement. But when Joan had her public spat with Johnny and announced her new late-night talk show on the Fox Network, the issue was once again raised. And it didn't help matters that David Brenner, once another heir apparent, also embarked on a show of his own. One by one, Johnny Carson seems to be outlasting all his potential replacements.

Is David Letterman one of them? At this point, it is almost certain that you'll never see Dave simply move into Johnny's chair. After all, Dave has his own style, and his own following. He likes to joke that, during the period of the famous Carson alimony battle, Johnny asked him if he could come on Dave's show as his replacement. It makes about as much sense . . . I mean, can you seriously imagine Dave schmoozing it up with Ed McMahon and trading show biz quips with Doc Severinson? David Letterman doesn't even belong on the same stage as Doc's suits. The idea is grotesque.

But what might make more sense is that when Johnny Carson is really ready to retire (and the Lord only knows when that will be), *The Tonight Show* can gracefully bow out of existence and leave the eleven-thirty slot open for *Late Night*. The chances are very good that if Johnny decides to vacate that time slot it would be offered to Dave. Producer Fred de Cordova says, "I know Johnny often watches *Late Night* and continues to think David is very talented. We're very fond of him here." One night when some piece of Carson's material was bombing, he joked, "Why don't I just go on home and we can bring in Letterman now." Yes, Dave has Johnny's blessing and equally to the point, he has Carson as a partner in his production company.

Would David take the job? Should he? He has his doubts. "Our show wouldn't work in prime time because viewer expectation is different. They want *Dallas* and

Dynasty. Completely detailed shows. We just do a sort of sloppy hour. We wouldn't do as well at eleven-thirty because there are too many natural obstacles. One of them is a guy who's been on at that hour for twenty-two years. People would be standing in line to make comparisons. Network executives would come out of the woodwork—that's where they keep them—and immigrants from Albania who just arrived in this country would say I wasn't as good as Johnny." It may well be the case that twelve-thirty really is the natural home of the *Late Night* show. It's a time that seems to be convenient for most of the hard-core audience. (*Why* these people are up and at loose ends between 12:30 and 1:30 a.m. is another question entirely.) Most of the people who tell you, "I really don't think David Letterman is that funny" then go on to add that they never stay up that late anyway. So there seems to be some sort of process of natural selection whereby only the people who find Dave amusing are up to watch him, or vice versa. This delicate balance might be upset by a move to an earlier time slot.

On the other hand, it might turn out to be the case that exposure to a wider audience would win David Letterman more fans. *Late Night* is not a good show to drop in on once in a blue moon. You see a little nerd in a Hawaiian shirt playing the piano and saying, "I know I'm really excited" about some guest whose claim to fame is working in a steakhouse in Nebraska; people come out and demonstrate how their dog can balance a cracker on its nose; then there's a commercial for a show called "The New Regulator Guy." What's a sane person to think?

An earlier time slot might allow more people the chance to get familiar with the David Letterman perspective and therefore ultimately to become fans. With his mainstream cultural values and his nice-guy personality, he has "the right stuff" to be popular with the audience that tunes in at eleven-thirty. You have to bear in mind that he *was* well liked as a guest host on Carson, and with the scope to do things his own way, he might win over even more viewers. Then, with eleven-thirty secure against the challengers, NBC could give David's old slot to some other up-and-coming sort who would eventually become the subject of a lot of speculation about whether or not he would be David Letterman's replacement when Dave retires.

Or then there's always the chance that Dave doesn't have Johnny Carson's stamina and won't choose to be on the air for twenty-plus years. Sometime in the next few years, he might conclude that he has accomplished what he set out to do, that he is bored by doing the same thing over and over, and that it is time for him to move on to something else. What might that be? Well, he might stay in television but opt out of the grind of a daily show. He would surely be welcome to write and star in a comedy special periodically, to appear as a guest or guest host on other stars' shows, perhaps even to do a limited series. Steve Allen's career might be a good model: he makes a guest appearance every now and then, had that series on PBS called *Meeting of Minds* about the great thinkers of the ages, and then hosted *The Start of Something Big*, a curious combination of trivia, gossip-oriented magazine segments, and little comedy bits by Steve. In other words, it was more or less tailored to his talents, and no doubt some sponsor would be happy to underwrite something of the sort for David Letterman.

Another possibility is the sit-com route. Dave and Merrill did once think about writing one, you recall, and they might even like to try one that didn't star David Letterman. Anyone who had the wit to cast Calvert DeForest as Larry "Bud" Melman could probably do a whale of a job with a family sit-com. Of course, there's also the option of creating the sit-com as a vehicle for Dave, but then it's hard to picture him deliberately putting himself in the position where he has to act every week of his life.

But why stay in television at all? Maybe David Letterman is ready to go on to the movies. He might choose to write and direct, with some help from Merrill and the other professionals with whom he has worked in television. Moviemaking might be a logical extension of his career, breaking out of the limitations inherent in television formats and allowing himself the freedom of more time, no interruptions, and the chance to develop his comic ideas in more depth. Talk of a David Letterman movie is already in the air; only time will tell how seriously the possibility is being considered, not only by David himself, but also by the studio heads, independent producers, and financial backers who are the real powers in today's Hollywood. Manager Jack Rollins probably knows exactly how to connect Dave with the right people; he does, after all, manage Woody Allen too.

In his 1982 interview with Debbie Paul, Dave mentioned his interest in developing his talent in a different direction. "To me, nothing would be greater than to have a regular print outlet on a magazine or newspaper. Authors like Robert Benchley and S. J. Perelman are still with us although they are long gone. Tell me who produced *Bosom Buddies* last week. It's a whole different situation. My first love has always been writing short essays. If I thought I had an outlet for that now I'd jump at it in a second. . . . I can get a meeting with Norman Lear tomorrow, but I can't get anybody at *The New Yorker* to read my articles." Certainly that situation has changed by now. If Dave wanted to submit articles to any magazine, they would surely get a reading. *Esquire* or the *Village Voice* or *GQ* might be happy to give him a regular column. He might even, like Garrison Keillor, write a book and hope to see it hit the best-seller list. He might be a bit surprised to find out how little one is paid for writing deathless prose compared to turning out even the most forgettable television show—but presumably he wouldn't be doing it for the money anyway.

One last possibility that shouldn't be overlooked is that David Letterman might like to take some time off simply to *live*. He probably can't remember the time when he hasn't been occupied with earning a living or building a career or both. It might be restful to take some time to do nothing but enjoy himself. He might get married, start a family, play softball a couple of times a week, romp with the dogs, build the kids a tree house. He's been earning a salary estimated to be in the high six figures for at least five years now, and much of that money has been sensibly invested to provide for his future (there's only so much you can spend buying new tires for your old pickup). He might take an interest in managing his money, or he might consider using it to start some congenial business venture. For example, a group of sports-minded businessmen are trying to bring a major league baseball team to Indianapolis: there's an investment tailor-made for David Letterman.

Letterman fans, of course, hope that he will continue to find some public forum for his comedic talents; it would be a shame for them to be restricted to a few guys he plays softball with or talks to about the problems of owning a ball club.

But knowing Dave's taste for the unexpected, they are prepared to be surprised.

From the stage, screen and TV—Celebrities you want to read about!

THE REAL STORY
True-life accounts from
The Berkley Publishing Group

_____ **BREAKING POINTS**   0-425-08784-0/$3.95
by Jack & Jo Ann Hinckley with Elizabeth Sherrill
The painful, probing story of their son's mental illness by
the parents of John Hinckley, Jr., the man who shot President
Ronald Reagan.

_____ **DAVID**   0-425-08766-2/$3.95
by Marie Rothenberg & Mel White
On March 3, 1983, David Rothenberg's father set fire to
the room where his son lay sleeping. Here is the story of his
remarkable recovery as seen through the eyes of his mother.

_____ **MASK**   0-425-07783-7/$2.95
a novel by John Minahan .
based on a screen play by Anna Hamilton Phelan
A moving, true-life story of a bright, 15-year-old boy who
suffers from a disfiguring disease, and the mother whose love
wouldn't die. An unforgettable motion picture starring Cher.

_____ **THE MICK**   0-515-08599-5/$3.95
by Mickey Mantle & Herb Gluck
The bestselling autobiography of America's baseball legend.

_____ **CLOSE ENCOUNTERS**   0-425-08269-5/$4.95
MIKE WALLACE'S OWN STORY
by Mike Wallace and Gary Paul Gates
"This is the real Mike Wallace." —Dan Rather
A _New York Times_ bestseller!

_____ **AND SO IT GOES**   0-425-10237-8/$4.50
by Linda Ellerbee
"The absurdities of television news...witty and irreverent."
—New York Times

New York Times bestsellers— Books at their best!